"Ron and Judy Blue and Jeremy White are the 'go to' people for sound, Bible-based financial advice. *Your Kids Can Master Their Money* is a hands-on, real-world application of spiritual truths for every family. If you have kids you MUST read this book. It is fun, easy, and will disturb you to action with your kids. Great job!"

—DAVE RAMSEY
New York Times bestselling author
and nationally syndicated radio host

"I absolutely love *Your Kids Can Master Their Money*! This is my kind of book—I know *what* I'm supposed to be doing, I need someone to show me *how*. The combination of authors, Blue and White, have written a resource that is a perfect blend of philosophy and practicality."

—LISA WHELCHEL
Bestselling author of *Creative Correction*, *The Facts of Life and Other Lessons My Father Taught Me*, and *Taking Care of the 'Me' in Mommy*

"The tips in this exciting, new book are fun and doable, while the financial advice is as rock-solid as ever. The result of melding this book's advice with its fun activities is a positive, eternal payback for our kids. If the number one reason for divorce is "arguments over money," then the single best thing we can do for our kids' futures is to help them master their money; *Your Kids Can Master Their Money* shows us how."

—ELLIE KAY
America's Family Financial Expert™, national radio commentator with *Money Matters*, and bestselling author of eight books

"Biblically sound and fun to read, this book is for parents who want to teach money management skills to their kids and won't mind learning a little something along the way for themselves, too."

—MARY HUNT
Author of *Debt-Proof Your Kids*

"Ron Blue gets to the heart of financial issues in simple ways that children can understand. This book will be very beneficial to parents as they work to teach their children integrity in their financial futures."

—SALLY CLARKSON
Whole Heart Ministries

FOCUS ON THE FAMILY
RESOURCES

Your Kids Can Master Their Money

FUN WAYS TO HELP THEM LEARN HOW

RON and JUDY BLUE
JEREMY WHITE

Tyndale House Publishers, Inc.
Carol Stream, Illinois

Library of Congress Cataloging-in-Publication Data
Blue, Ron, 1942-
  Your kids can master their money : fun ways to help them learn how / Ron
and Judy Blue and Jeremy White.
      p. cm.
  "A Focus on the Family book."
  Includes bibliographical references.
  ISBN-13: 978-1-58997-191-2
  ISBN-10: 1-58997-191-4
  1. Children—Finance, Personal. 2. Teenagers—Finance, Personal. 3. Saving and
investment. 4. Child rearing—Economic aspects. 5. Finance, Personal—Religious
aspects—Christianity. I. Blue, Judy, 1944- II. White, Jeremy (Jeremy L.) III. Title.
  HG179.B5662 2006
  332.0240083—dc22
                                              2006004821

Printed in the United States of America
  2 3 4 5 6 7 8 9 /11 10 09 08 07 06

Judy and I want to dedicate this book to our parents, who modeled financial responsibility—and to our children, Cynthia, Denise, Karen, Tim, and Michael, who daily modeled teachability as they were growing up.

—Ron and Judy Blue

I dedicate this book to my parents, Jerrell and Connie White. May I pass on their wisdom and character to my children.

—Jeremy White

Acknowledgments

We owe a deep debt of gratitude to our five children, who taught us much about responsibility and maturity as we watched them grow up. Today they are not only responsible money managers but, more importantly, in every case responsible parents who are in turn modeling and teaching their children.

We also very much appreciate the friendship, counsel, and wisdom from our agent, Robert Wolgemuth. He, with great care, mentored us along in the whole process. We appreciate him very much.

We also want to acknowledge our relationship with Jeremy White, who has been a joy to work with over the last several years on multiple projects. There could be no one better as a co-author than Jeremy White.

Lastly we, like millions of others, have been deeply impacted by the wisdom of Dr. James Dobson. Much of what we know about parenting came from his teaching. God has used him mightily in our generation, and to call him a friend is a deep privilege.

—*Ron and Judy Blue*

Like many adults traveling on the journey of parenting, I acknowledge my inadequacy as a parent. I suppose God is still honing and shaping us as parents. That's why parenting is so tough. With my professional financial background, I'm comfortable in the financial realm. But applying that financial knowledge—or any knowledge—to help your own children is a challenge.

I could not have arrived at this point without Sharon, my parenting partner and life companion. She is my sounding board, prayer warrior, motivator, balancer, and encourager. How I enjoy the journey with her!

The activities in this book have been kid-tested by our daughters, Jenaye and Jaclyn. They have graciously put up with many of Dad's money games, planning ideas, and money lectures. The readers and kids out there should thank them for helping to eliminate some of the not-so-fun activities that were left out of this book.

I would also like to thank Ron Blue for his wisdom that oozes out with such ease. With a humorous and gentle humility, he helps me and so many others reduce the complex to the simple essentials.

People often ask me how I find time to write books and maintain a full-time accounting and investment practice. It's only possible by God's empowerment and a great support team of Kris White, Pam Estes, and Todd White. You three are such valuable co-laborers for these big writing projects. Thank you for your patience and editing.

—*Jeremy White*

Contents

How and Why to Use This Book

Emily wastes more money at the mall costume jewelry store on cheap accessories than you made in an entire summer mowing yards when you were her age.

Jacob begs and manipulates you for every new electronic gadget for the computer and game console. You're not even sure what some of these things do! Resourceful, but unwise, Jacob simply advises you to whip out the plastic.

Nichole saves her best tantrums and pouting lips for the checkout lane when she doesn't get her sweet tooth satisfied.

Michael just added a few more gray hairs and wrinkles to your collection when he told you his intentions to quit college after one year. He has to work to pay off his credit card debts. He didn't handle wisely the numerous credit card offers and opportunities for late-night pizza.

Whew! How can you equip your children to survive financially? How can you reduce the conflicts in your family over endless requests to buy things? How can you get your children interested in saving and giving rather than only spending?

You're the most important teacher of your children. The tools and activities we provide in this book will empower you and your kids—not just to survive, but to thrive financially!

After researching many books designed to help parents teach their kids about money, we noticed a common outline in all of them. They make the same points:

- Parents have to model good money management.
- Kids need character to manage money well, and parents must teach character.
- Parents must consciously teach their kids to save, give, and spend wisely.

We don't disagree with the above points, but most books fall short. They don't tell you *how* to teach your kids. They say you *should* teach your kids. If you're able to finish these books, you often feel frustrated and perhaps guilty that you haven't done more. If they do tell you how, such application is buried in a long narrative.

As we wrote this book, we tapped into what we know professionally and what we understand about modern family life. We understand it because we live in the same world you do.

First, we're aware of how busy you and your kids are. The pace of life has been hectic for decades. Recently, though, the busyness barometer has shattered records. As author Tim Kimmel has noted, the norm for most families is "Little House on the Freeway," not the tranquility of prairie life. Many everyday conversations start with "Oh, we're just so busy!" Instead of asking people how they are, many ask, "Are you keeping busy?"

Second, we know that parenting is tough. Ron and Judy raised five children to adulthood and now watch their seven grandchildren grow up. Jeremy and his wife, Sharon, are raising and home-schooling their two daughters in the Internet age. Nothing is more gut-wrenching yet purifying, more heart-breaking yet heart-building, more demanding yet satisfying than parenting.

Practically every social challenge debated today, from drug use among teens to lower test scores to obesity, leads people to conclude, "Well, it all comes down to the family," or "It's up to the parents." You have so much to teach your children.

Others are trying to teach your kids about money—advertisers on Saturday morning TV, bazaars on the Internet, moviemakers using "kids' meal" tie-in promotions, discount store toy aisles, credit card companies. They all know how to focus on your kids' hearts and minds. They all hope to hit the bull's-eye and end up with some of your child's piggy bank savings—and some of your wallet. Marketers know that kids influence the spending of billions of dollars.

You may not feel capable or qualified to teach your children about money, but you can do it. Even though you may not have a degree in finance or accounting, or may not have balanced your checkbook in a few months, you *can* train your kids with meaningful activities. You may learn some new habits in the process, too.

We know. We've seen the key principles to financial success benefit the lives of many clients and their children. We've also seen how ignoring these principles brings financial heartaches for years to come. We've talked about them on the radio, at conferences, and on TV. We've written about them for years. These principles are straightforward and communicable.

Part I of the book is intended to provide you with the "why" of teaching, plus detailed information to equip you as a mentor. Part I will help make your methods more effective. For example, in Chapter 3, "Talking the Talk," we discuss how using clichés may hinder your effectiveness as a teacher, what financial data should not be discussed with children at various ages, and how your language should include financial and business terminology.

Still, if you never read a chapter in Part I, you'll benefit from the activities in Part II.

The heart of this book, Part II, was inspired by our application of key financial principles with our children. Here we offer projects, games, incentives, and challenges (we'll refer to all of these as "activities") to help you teach your kids financial wisdom.

Your family calendar probably doesn't have room for a dissertation about money management. So we designed the activities to be fun and engaging, enabling you to teach your children as you do the errands of life. You'll find activities that encourage the win-win experience of having fun with your kids and teaching them something, too.

You can pick the activities that will work best for your family. Every child is unique. No family is static; we're all moving through life. Instead of following our directions verbatim, adapt the activities for your family. Perhaps one of our plans will spark another idea, or you'll want to add a twist to our suggestion.

In Chapter 4 we've included our biggest and best idea. The envelope activity presented there efficiently teaches many of the skills necessary to become a money-smart kid. We've set it apart to discuss in more detail.

To help you with specific issues, we've provided "Here's My Challenge" in Part III. In a question-and-answer format we present real-life dilemmas, like one child taking financial advantage of another or grandparents giving too many gifts. Then we present a solution and the principles involved, referring back to an activity and sometimes suggesting a twist on it.

While we'd be grateful if you read the book cover to cover, we think you can best use it as a reference guide. Don't get bogged down in the many activities. Pull this book out when there's a character trait you want to emphasize, to obtain age-appropriate ideas, or to help with challenges you face.

Let's get started with why this job of teaching children about money falls to you.

PART I

Equipping You

Financial Pep Talk for Parents

From a Child's Perspective:
Art Linkletter once asked a four-year-old boy, "What do
    you want to be when you grow up?"
"I don't want to be anything," the boy replied.
"Don't you want to get married?"
"If I have to."
"And how will you get money?"
"My wife can work."
"But suppose she won't?"
"I'll send for my mother."[1]

*What are some surefire ways to make a person fall in love
    with you?*
"Tell them that you own a whole bunch of candy stores."
—DEL, AGE 6

Biblical Principles:
*He must manage his own family well and see that his children obey him
with proper respect. (If anyone does not know how to manage his own
family, how can he take care of God's church?)*—1 TIMOTHY 3:4-5

Discipline your son, and he will give you peace; he will bring delight to your soul.—PROVERBS 29:17

You're already on the right track.

By starting to read this book aimed at equipping parents to teach financial principles to their kids, you're acknowledging your role. Whether you like it or not, as a parent you realize you have some role in teaching your kids financial principles. Somehow, somewhere, in some way, you've sensed that raising money-smart kids is important.

Perhaps you want your kids to avoid some of the financial struggles you've experienced.

Perhaps you're tired of fighting the daily dollar battles with your kids. Your son expects you to spend big bucks on name-brand athletic shoes. Your daughter thinks she's entitled to designer clothes because "everyone else" has them. You're tired of your kids begging to order the most expensive item in the restaurant *plus* an appetizer and dessert.

Perhaps you realize that financial wisdom will help your child in so many areas of his or her future. A major factor in most divorces is poor financial management and the resulting stress. Many people are stuck in jobs they don't enjoy because they're trapped by their poor financial decisions. Many Christians aren't experiencing spiritual maturity and the joy of giving because they're "slave to the lender."

Perhaps you know you have some self-interest in this matter. A big motivation for parents is to avoid "boomerang kids." After enjoying an empty nest for a while, you don't want it to be filled again with 27-year-old birds who should be flying on their own. As our friend the late Larry Burkett said, "I wonder if parents would be more serious about teaching their kids financial principles if they realized their kids would be choosing and paying for their nursing home someday!"

The statistics show you're on the right track. The evidence is clear. Five powerful trends, supported by many studies and surveys, point toward the necessity of teaching the next generation the truth about financial principles. (Note: Unless otherwise stated, the following figures apply to the U.S.)

Trend #1: Financial illiteracy is the norm among America's youth.

- A Visa survey found that 49 percent of youth think they're more likely to become millionaires by starring in a reality TV series than by learning how to budget and save wisely.
- A *Consumer Reports* survey found 28 percent of students didn't know credit cards are a form of borrowing, and 40 percent didn't know that banks charge interest on loans.
- The National Center on Education and the Economy found that nearly two-thirds of American adults and students didn't know that in times of inflation, money loses its value.
- Between 1990 and 1999, there was a 51 percent increase in annual bankruptcy filings among adults 25 years of age and younger.

Trend #2: Kids and teens have money and spending influence—and advertisers and credit card companies are coming after them.

- MarketResearch.com reports that in 2003, teens spent $175 billion, averaging $103 per week. The so-called "tweens," 8-to-14-year-olds, spent $39 billion in 2003.
- Younger kids directly influence the spending decisions on their behalf to the tune of $117 billion.
- Marketers target children as young as 18 months.[2]
- By the time your kids reach 21, they'll have seen or heard an estimated 23 million advertising "impressions."[3]
- One consumer-marketing group reported that today's kids will have seen 360,000 30-second TV commercials by the time they're 20 years old.

- One-third of high school seniors use a credit card. Not surprisingly, seniors who used a credit card scored significantly lower on a national, personal finance literacy survey than seniors who didn't use a card.[4]
- More than three-fourths of college undergraduate students have credit cards; most have multiple cards with an average unpaid balance of $2,748. Ninety-five percent of college graduate students have cards; each has an average of four cards with an average unpaid balance of $4,776.

Trend #3: Parents apparently presume someone else is teaching kids about money and finances.

- Eighty percent of parents surveyed believed that schools provided classes on money management and budgeting.
- Only seven states require students to complete a course that includes personal finance before graduating from high school.[5] As a comparison, sex education is taught in 90 percent of public schools starting in fifth grade; it's a required course for 69 percent of schools.[6]
- Much of the limited curriculum available in schools is provided at no charge from various education coalitions. Usually the main funding sources of these coalitions are Visa, American Express, or other credit card companies (not exactly the most impartial source of wisdom).
- Pastors are frequently silent on the topics of money and stewardship.
- Very few evangelical churches have active stewardship discipleship courses for equipping young people to handle money from God's perspective.

Trend #4: Whether parents like it or not—or even realize it—kids look to them for financial guidance.

- The American Savings Education Council found that 94 percent of kids turn to their parents for financial information.

- Sixty-three percent of older teenagers, notorious for knowing it all and not listening to parents, say they get *most* of their information on money matters from their parents.[7]
- The Financial Educational Survey by Capital One found that more than 70 percent of parents say they have spoken with their teens about credit and using credit cards wisely; less than 44 percent of the teenage children of those respondents say their parents have talked to them about credit cards. Meanwhile, 54 percent of parents rate their teenagers' knowledge about managing money as "good" or "excellent," while an overwhelming 78 percent of the teenage children of those respondents rated their knowledge as merely average or even poor.
- The Jump$tart Coalition survey found that only 26 percent of 13- to 21-year-olds reported that their parents actively taught them how to manage money.

Trend #5: Financial support to churches and ministries is tenuous at present—and likely to be even weaker in the future.

- One study estimated that most church giving comes from people over age 55.
- Barna Research Group found the following in its 2003 survey of giving in churches: The mean amount of money donated to churches and other worship centers in 2003 was $824. This is less than the inflation-adjusted amount for 2000. The segments that were *least likely* to tithe included adults under 35 and those from households with a gross income of $40,000 to $59,999.
- Howard Dayton, CEO of Crown Financial Ministries, has stated that many pastors have told him most of their giving comes from members over 65. They estimate that it takes five people under age 35 to replace one senior's giving.

The evidence is clear: Kids need financial training, and they need it from you.

We know you have urgent tasks on your to-do list: chauffeuring your kids to the next music lesson, attending their next ball game, trying to get them to do their homework, and prying them off the Internet. Such is the tyranny of the urgent in modern life. The ringing phone and the broken garage door opener tug us away from the truly important, eternal issues like daily prayer time and nurturing our children. Our aim in this book is to help you complete the truly important task of equipping your children to do well in an area crucial to success—wise money management.

How do you teach your kids to master their money? How can they be generous givers, sharp shoppers, savvy savers, prudent planners, intelligent investors, and willing workers?

Kids learn about money from you as parents and from their own experiences. Notice that we didn't say they learn much at school. How ironic that they go to school to learn how to be successful in life, but don't learn how to manage money wisely! In fact, the mere act of going to advanced schooling may result in huge student loan debts.

When your kids learn from you, you're either teaching intentionally or inadvertently—the latter through the habits they observe. Teaching intentionally is better. You do that by sharing truths "as you go" or by creating experiences that help kids learn. Let's look at these methods a bit more closely.

As You Go

An efficient approach to help your kids become financially mature is to teach them "as you go." The lecture method rarely works at home, anyway. Parents think they make good speeches, but kids don't agree.

You may think that we authors are financial nerds who'd enjoy sitting down on a Saturday night for two hours and discussing with our children the benefits of budgeting. We wouldn't. We can assure you that our kids wouldn't enjoy such a session, either.

God recognized that the Israelites best taught their children as they "went along." The basis for this method is found in Deuteronomy 6:4-9:

> *Hear, O Israel: the LORD our God, the LORD is one. Love the LORD your God with all your heart and with all your soul and with all your strength. These commandments that I give you today are to be upon your hearts. Impress them on your children. Talk about them when you sit at home and when you walk along the road, when you lie down and when you get up. Tie them as symbols on your hands and bind them on your foreheads. Write them on the doorframes of your houses and on your gates.*

The instruction was to parents. Parents should impress upon their children the commandments and truths of God as they go along. If we were to reword these verses in a more modern translation, we might say the following:

> *Talk about them when you sit at the dinner table and at family devotions and when you drive along the highway, when you are tucking them in at night and when you are at the breakfast table and driving them to school. Write them as Post-it notes on your mirrors and pin them to the corkboards in your kitchen.*

Many of the activities we've included in this book can be taught as you go. For example, the "Advertising Detectives" game can be played as you're watching a ball game on TV or as you're driving down the road and seeing billboards. The financial board games can be played during the family time you were planning to have anyway. Use some "Sharp Shopper" activities when you're at the store with your kids.

Jesus continually taught His disciples as they went along. In the middle of a field, in the temple, or at sea in a boat, He used events to teach them. Look at the following excerpts from the Gospels. These are just a few examples of many teachings introduced by the phrases "As they went along" or "During everyday happenings."

As they were walking along the road, a man said to him . . . (Luke 9:57)

As Jesus and his disciples were on their way, he came to a village where a woman named Martha opened her home to him. (Luke 10:38)

One day Jesus was praying in a certain place. When he finished, one of his disciples said to him, "Lord, teach us to pray, just as John taught his disciples." (Luke 11:1)

Then Jesus went through the towns and villages, teaching as he made his way to Jerusalem. (Luke 13:22)

Now on his way to Jerusalem, Jesus traveled along the border between Samaria and Galilee. As he was going into a village, ten men who had leprosy met him. (Luke 17:11-12)

As Jesus approached Jericho, a blind man was sitting by the roadside begging. (Luke 18:35)

As he looked up, Jesus saw the rich putting their gifts into the temple treasury. He also saw a poor widow. . . . (Luke 21:1-2)

Some of his disciples were remarking about how the temple was adorned with beautiful stones and with gifts dedicated to God. But Jesus said . . . (Luke 21:5)

These are just a few of the many times Jesus took advantage of teachable moments. He even used arguing and bickering among the disciples: *"An argument started among the disciples as to which of them would be the greatest. Jesus, knowing their thoughts, took a little child and had him stand beside him"* (Luke 9:46-47).

On another occasion, *"a dispute arose among them as to which of them was considered to be greatest*" (Luke 22:24). Jesus overheard His disciples and used that moment to instruct them.

Maybe your kids never bicker. But if they do, follow Christ's example and use their quarreling as an opportunity to teach. Learning occurs when the pupil is willing and can relate to what the teacher is offering *then*. This is especially true when teaching children. Children are best taught as you go—as you go to the bank, as you go on vacation, as you go to church, as you go to the grocery, as you're buying gas. We don't want you to miss those great teachable moments.

We heard a story from a client who wondered why one child always lingered behind when the family was leaving restaurants on vacation. When confronted, the child produced a pocketful of change and dollar bills. He'd thought his parents were carelessly leaving money behind, and he was going to collect it!

Now *there* was a teachable moment.

You don't have to wait for your child to grab a gratuity, though, to deliver a lesson on the subject. As you're leaving a tip, explain how a waitress earns her money. Explain how it's customary for patrons of sit-down restaurants to leave a percentage.

The same is true when other opportunities present themselves. As you drive through a tollbooth, explain how users pay for certain roads or bridges. As you renew your license plate tags, explain special use taxes.

If you try to teach your children financial principles by sitting them down and saying, "Now you're going to learn how to buy a shirt wisely," you won't succeed. The best way to learn about money is to have experiences with it—in this case, to buy a shirt and to hear your feedback.

To teach your children "as you go" requires that you listen to them. When we say "listen," we don't mean only to hear their words. Listen to the meanings and feelings behind the words. What are they really saying? Why are they saying it? How can you best respond in word pictures or examples they can understand?

This type of listening means you're tuned into them, not into what's going on at work or what's on the calendar for tonight or tomorrow. It means being where they are mentally as well as physically.

Without this active listening, we'll miss the most teachable moments. We each confess that in our homes, our wives are the better listeners and teachers. It requires a constant choice on our part to listen to what our kids are really saying. We find that when we do, we're able to teach in the daily course of life. Very seldom in such instances have we set out to teach something on purpose. It's just happened "as we go."

Creating Teachable Times

To provide other learning opportunities, you can arrange situations, set up games, or create "test labs" before your kids wade into the "real world." To teach a 14-year-old daughter about the stock market, for example, we recommend an activity using a simulation of choosing stocks and tracking them on paper (see Chapter 10). This will provide some learning before she plunks down $500 of her babysitting money.

To help your children appreciate their standard of living compared to the rest of the world, meanwhile, we have an activity called "Candy, Dolls, Army Men, and Proportions" (see Chapter 6).

Learning experiences take a bit of effort, but they're worth it. It isn't necessary to learn every lesson the hard way. If you can create experiences, mentor your kids through them, and evaluate the results, your children will be better prepared to handle real-life situations on their own.

If we look at how Jesus trained His disciples, we can learn four principles for training children in all areas, including money management.

1. They must experience what is being taught.
2. They must have an opportunity to fail.

3. They must have feedback.
4. They must have rewards.

The activities in this book that you choose to adapt to your family will reinforce some or all of these principles. The process is like teaching a skill such as waterskiing.

All five of our (Blue family) children have learned to water ski. Waterskiing appears to be a fairly simple physical activity, and it's easy to explain how you learn to get up on those narrow slats. You merely keep your weight behind the skis and let the boat pull you out of the water. You *must* let the boat do all the work.

They must experience what is being taught

Waterskiing may be easy to explain, but it took us hours and hours of attempts before our children could get up on the water. After they learned to get up, however, the second time was easy—and the third was even easier. Only then did the sport become their own. Money management is the same way.

It's easy to tell your children that they should tithe, save, and spend wisely. But until they experience the joy of tithing, the rewards of having saved for a major purchase, and the thrill of seeing how much money they've saved by being smart shoppers, telling them means nothing. The training process must give them an opportunity to experience what you're attempting to teach them. Only by allowing your children to experience what you're telling them will the principle and practice become theirs. It's at this point that training has occurred.

They must have an opportunity to fail

If we hadn't given our children the freedom to fail while learning to ski, they wouldn't have tried. Your kids will fail at times—just as ours have. Just as you have.

Failure is a part of life and learning. The issue is not whether children will fail, but how they'll respond to failure. The best time for them to fail is while they're young, and parents are available to counsel them.

Probably the biggest mistake parents make in training children to manage money is not giving them the freedom to fail. Parents either make decisions for them or are so critical of their decisions that children quickly learn not to risk anything on their own.

They must have feedback

Waterskiing provides clear feedback: If you stay up, you succeeded. If your posterior remains underwater or you get up briefly only to greet the water face-first, you know you have more skills to learn.

Similarly, as you use experiences to teach your children financial principles, they'll need your verbal feedback or other means of letting them know how they're doing.

They must have rewards

You can leverage your kids' learning by offering monetary rewards or privilege incentives based on their achievement.

Jesus used the promise of rewards—and warnings of lost rewards—to motivate His disciples as well as today's believers. Rewards are biblical, they're motivational, and they provide a source of feedback.

We've given many types of rewards to our children through the years. The simplest approach is merely giving them a star for a particular behavior, such as cleaning their room; we had a chart on the refrigerator that was used just for this purpose.

Praise, given privately or in front of the rest of the family, is another type of reward. So is individual time with a parent. An occasional treat or privilege can also be used.

Money has also been a reward. We're cautious about this, though, because it can easily become a form of bribery—a convenient way to manipulate a child for our own benefit. Still, we've used it when it seemed like a good way to encourage a child to choose to do the right thing.

One of those times came when our (the Blues) second daughter, Denise, decided to take up basketball as a junior in high school. That year she set a school rebounding record, but her shooting percentage was very low. The summer before her senior year I (Ron) challenged her to shoot 50 shots a day. I promised a monetary reward at the end of the summer for the number of shots taken. This seemed a good way to motivate her and to teach her the benefits of self-discipline. She completed the shots for the summer and received the reward.

During her senior year, she was second on the team in free throw percentage. During a crucial game, she was called upon to shoot a technical foul. At that point in the season, she had the highest free throw percentage on the team. She made the pressure-filled shot! Because she'd worked hard, she was able to achieve a new level of performance. She was really doubly rewarded.

In addition to offering rewards, consider withholding them as a motivational tool. One of the training techniques we've used is giving the reward ahead of time—and taking it away if the desired behavior is not followed.

For example, we (the Blues) were having trouble with the children being critical of one another, especially at dinnertime. After giving the matter some thought, we handed each of them a jar containing $10 in quarters. We told them that for the next 30 days, any time we heard a criticism we would remove a quarter from the jar of the child who made the remark, without exception. We made it clear that they could have the quarters remaining at the end of that period. It didn't take more than two days for the criticism to stop!

We believe that was much more effective than if we'd said, "If you don't criticize, we'll give you $10 at the end of a month." Again, we used a reward as a motivator and a form of feedback rather than as a bribe.

How would you prefer your kids develop their financial skills, form their beliefs about money, and plan their future: from your intentional methods or from advertisements? Wouldn't you prefer to create teachable experiences with their own money instead of having them make decisions based on keeping up with their peers?

Your children will need to know much more than you ever did to survive and thrive financially. Think of the changes in the brief time since you were a kid: new ways of shopping via the Internet; new ways of saving for college through Education Savings Accounts, 529 plans, and prepaid tuition plans; debit cards and the decline in use of cash; credit card companies acting more aggressively in pursuing new and younger customers; the increased sophistication of advertisers; spam e-mail.

Alan Greenspan, former chairman of the Federal Reserve Bank, agreed: "Today's financial world is highly complex when compared with that of a generation ago. . . . Children and teenagers should begin learning basic financial skills as early as possible. Indeed, improving basic financial education can help prevent students from making poor decisions later, when they are young adults, that can take years to overcome."[8]

Even if you're on the right track, you'll still be run over if you just sit there. Getting moving with the activities in this book will help you and your family make sense of dollars and cents!

Your Reward as a Parent

Is the effort of teaching your children about money worth it? Don't just look at the cost—look at the benefits. We can think of four rewards for training children to be good stewards.

First of all, you can expect to stand before the Lord someday and hear His blessing, "Well done." Ultimately, your kids are responsible for the choices they make as adults. But if you've trained them to act as responsible and godly grown-ups, you can expect to hear Him say, *"Well done, good and faithful servant! You have been faithful with a few things; I will put you in charge of many things. Come and share your master's happiness"* (Matthew 25:21).

Second, you can expect your children to be good stewards of the resources God has entrusted to them. You can also expect to see them train their own children to manage financial resources in a godly, responsible manner.

We don't sense conflict among our (the Blues) kids regarding money. They all get along—despite 11 years difference between the oldest and youngest. They have all married spouses with a shared financial value system.

Those of us who've trained children and watched them go into the world have no greater reward than seeing them make wise decisions. The Blue children are not perfect, and we don't wish to put them or their financial positions on a pedestal. Many times we say to ourselves, "What happened? How did they learn to do that?" What a thrill it is to see children making good decisions! We simply use them as motivation and encouragement for you.

Third, we believe that when you enter this training process, you can expect to eliminate most of the conflict with children over money. That alone is sufficient reward for many parents to make the commitment. Shopping at Wal-Mart or stopping at the corner convenience store should not be a battle with your kids.

Fourth, you can expect to see your children, even in their pre-teen years, begin to make sound financial decisions. Good decisions about what clothes to wear, how to spend extra money, tithing, saving, and planning for the future are reasonable expectations when children have been trained in the way they should go. I (Jeremy) am thrilled to see my daughters prepare their offering each Sunday morning on their own and drop it in the plate cheerfully.

At no time are individuals more moldable than in childhood. Children generally want to learn what parents would have them learn. Sure, they may act stubborn or rebellious at times, but most are teachable. After they experience the rewards of self-discipline and wisdom, they'll gradually seek to make good decisions more often.

Parenting will challenge and stretch you beyond your limitations. But God is willing and able to supply all your needs.

Memorize and apply daily James 1:5, which states, *"If any of you lacks wisdom, he should ask God, who gives generously to all without finding fault, and it will be given to him."*

We don't have all the answers, but we know the Source who does. God is not only growing our children up, but He is growing us up as well. Each of us must ask continually what God would have us learn.

As you begin the great adventure of training your children to manage money, remember that God will guard and keep what you've committed to Him. Children are children, and mistakes tend to be the same from one generation to the next. God is far more able to meet our children's needs than we are, and far more concerned about the training responsibility than we are. He will provide us with what we need, when we need it, to train up His children in His ways.

This commitment to instruct may cost you some time, effort, and maybe a little money. But the costs are nothing compared to the prize. As we heard our late colleague and friend, Larry Burkett, say, "The investment of time in teaching biblical financial principles to the young generation will pay dividends for an eternity."

You and your kids can triumph against materialism and consumerism. You can discover a system that empowers you and your children to master your money God's way. Remember the success adage: Triumph is just "umph" added to "try."

Commit by faith to pay the price to train your children in the way they should go. When they get old, they won't depart from it. And you will rejoice as you see them *"live a life worthy of the Lord and . . . please him in every way"* (Colossians 1:10).

Walking the Walk

From a Child's Perspective:

Dear Pastor,

I'm sorry I can't leave more money in the plate, but my father didn't give me a raise in my allowance. Could you have a sermon about a raise in my allowance?

Love, Patty. Age 10, New Haven[1]

TEACHER: "If you had one dollar and you asked your father for another, how many dollars would you have?"

VINCENT: "One dollar."

TEACHER: (sadly) "You don't know your arithmetic."

VINCENT: (sadly) "You don't know my father."

Biblical Principles:

Two things I ask of you, O LORD; do not refuse me before I die: Keep falsehood and lies far from me; give me neither poverty nor riches, but give me only my daily bread. Otherwise, I may have too much and disown you and say, "Who is the LORD?"—PROVERBS 30: 7-9

But the wisdom that comes from heaven is first of all pure; then peaceloving, considerate, submissive, full of mercy and good fruit, impartial and sincere.—JAMES 3:17

In the 1700s two men developed distinct reputations for themselves.

One was Jonathan Edwards, a man of integrity, refinement, and Christian character.

The other, nicknamed "Max Juke" by the author who studied him, was a hard drinker who worked only sporadically.

A trace of Edwards' descendants in 1900 and one of Juke's family in 1877 proved interesting. In Jonathan Edwards' line were 13 college presidents; 100 clergymen, missionaries, and theology professors; 80 elected public officials; 60 physicians; 60 authors and editors; and practically no lawbreakers. On the other hand, Juke's descendants included 128 prostitutes, 140 criminals, and 67 who contracted a social disease.[2]

We have a choice. We can model good behavior or bad. The type of behavior we display will affect future generations. As Dr. Howard Hendricks of Dallas Theological Seminary repeatedly stated, "More is caught than taught."

Your children may not be the best listeners, but they're excellent imitators. We don't have to say a thing to our children to pass on to them our decisions, priorities, commitments, and habits. Where and how we spend money is influenced by how and where our parents spent money. Children will either emulate our behavior or react to it and behave in the opposite way.

For example, if your father bought a new car every year, chances are you'll do the same. If your parents always ate a Sunday meal out, you're likely to follow suit. If your parents paid cash for everything, you may find it difficult to use credit cards.

On the other hand, if you were always forced to wear second-hand clothes, you might determine that you'll always buy new clothing—and that your wardrobe will always represent the latest in fashion.

Just as your parents had an effect on you, you're having an

effect on your children. That can be a bit scary! They're watching everything.

One day a guy was driving with his four-year-old daughter and beeped his car horn by mistake. She turned and looked at him for an explanation.

He said, "I did that by accident."

She replied, "I know that, Daddy."

He replied, "How'd you know?"

The girl said, "Because you didn't say *jerk* afterwards."

As you begin intentionally instructing your kids, you may need to clean up your personal finances. Ron has written, with Jeremy's assistance, a book devoted to helping you clean up financial messes: *The New Master Your Money: A Step-by-Step Plan for Gaining and Enjoying Financial Freedom* (Moody Publishers, 2004). This practical guide takes the anxiety out of money matters and helps adults get their finances in order. In this chapter, we'll highlight some topics covered in greater depth by *The New Master Your Money*.

Several years ago, I (Ron) had the opportunity to testify before a Senate subcommittee that was holding hearings on "Solutions for the New Era: Jobs and Families." While others on the panel pressed for more social programs, I told the senators and their staffs that the average family could benefit from following a four-part financial plan:

1. Spend less than you earn.
2. Avoid the use of debt.
3. Maintain liquidity.
4. Set long-term goals.

The committee chairman listened carefully and recited the points back to me. He paused a moment, then said, "It seems like this plan is not just for the family. It seems it would work at any income level."

"Yes," I said with a laugh, "including the government."

What's good for the goose is good for the gander. These basic steps will work for the government and for your household. They'll work for you as parents and will work for your children.

Financial planning may sound overwhelming, like something that can only be practiced by professionals in suits. But it's pretty straightforward.

Simply stated, financial planning is allocating limited financial resources among various unlimited alternatives. When we know for certain what financial resources we have and plan to use them to accomplish God-given goals and objectives, we experience the peace and contentment that comes from making order out of chaos. Our frustration in having to choose among overwhelming choices disappears. We're freed from the pressures of the short-term, self-gratifying society around us. We're free to be different.

Most of us are responders rather than planners. We respond to friends, advertising, and our emotions rather than planning our spending. So here are the challenges of wise financial planning:

- All of us have limited resources. Consequently, we must be selective in how we spend our money.
- Today's decisions determine destiny. (A dollar spent is gone forever and can never be used in the future for anything else.)
- The more long-term the perspective, the better potential for wise decisions.

Objectives of Financial Planning

One principle we've implied but haven't actually stated is that accumulating financial resources should never be an end in itself. Money is accumulated solely for the reason of using it to accomplish some purpose.

For example, you don't take a vacation or buy a car just to spend money, but to provide something else such as recreation or transportation. Many people ask me (Ron) how to spend money. I always respond, "What are you really trying to accomplish?" This question helps to focus the decision on real objectives.

In the short term, there are basically only five spending objectives; in the long term, only six. Every spending decision or use of money accomplishes one of these eleven objectives.

Short-Term Objectives

Figure 1 illustrates that there are only five short-term uses for all household income:

1. Given away
2. Spent to support a lifestyle
3. Used for the repayment of debt
4. Used to meet tax obligations
5. Saved (cash flow margin)

Every spending decision, in the short term, will fit into one of these five categories.

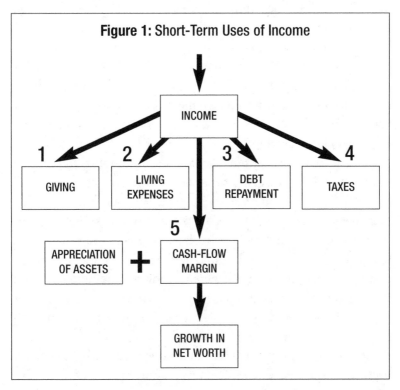

Figure 1: Short-Term Uses of Income

How your money is allocated among the five categories is determined by just two factors: the commitments you already have, and your priorities. For example, with five children, we (Ron and Judy) had certain lifestyle commitments, including debt repayment, taxes, and giving—as well as insurance, utilities, and other household expenses—that we were obligated to maintain. As time passed, our financial obligations to those commitments changed as our family situation and my career changed.

Ultimately, after our commitments have been met, our priorities dictate the use of our remaining resources. Giving and saving are usually stated as priorities, but in reality, they often wind up at the bottom of our priority ladder. We've observed that most Christians in prosperous western countries have lifestyle as their top priority. The second priority, because of their lifestyle, is debt repayment. Taxes would be a third priority because they have no choice; fourth would be saving; and finally, giving.

The line of reasoning goes this way: "I am already committed to a certain lifestyle and debt schedule, which God surely wouldn't want me to change. I would gladly give up paying my taxes, but I can't. I am giving and would give more if it weren't for the taxes I have to pay and the money I need to set aside for the future because that is good stewardship."

Of the five short-term uses, three are consumptive and two are productive. Lifestyle expenditures, debt repayment, and taxes are all consumptive; when the money is spent, it's gone forever. Saving and giving, on the other hand, are productive uses of money. Saving is much like planting a crop—later on, much more than what was planted comes up and can be used again for either consumption or production. Giving benefits you now with joy and later with eternal rewards; giving also benefits others now.

The Bible gives us many principles and guidelines about each of these five areas, but very little in the way of direct commandment. To determine what God would have us do in balancing our priorities requires the discipline of spending time with Him. No one other person, including your financial planner, can tell you how to prioritize your spending. Why? God has not entrusted the resources you possess to someone else; only you are accountable for managing the use of God's resources entrusted to you.

Long-Term Objectives

In reviewing Figure 2, you'll note that as we save from our cash flow margin, we grow our net worth—not for the sake of big numbers, but for the purpose of meeting one of our long-term objectives. Common long-term objectives include the following:

1. Financial independence
2. College education for children
3. Major charitable giving
4. Major lifestyle desires
5. Paying off debt
6. Owning your own business

To be financially independent means that the resources accumulated will generate enough income to fund all the short-term objectives during your lifespan, with the exception of savings. (Savings are no longer needed if "enough" has been accumulated.) When people know what their short-term objectives are, they can easily calculate how large an investment fund is necessary to accumulate what they need in order to be financially independent.

In addition to accumulating for financial independence, couples with children often have the long-term objective of helping to pay for their college education. Teenagers may contribute toward college expenses through their own work and savings, but many parents want to limit the amount of student loan debt their children incur. Saving and wise investing usually are necessary in order to afford a college education—an expense that can easily reach $15,000 to $20,000 per year for each child.

When it comes to the long-term goal of giving, consider giving strategically and intentionally—not just out of money that's left over. One of the first clients with whom I (Ron) worked was a man

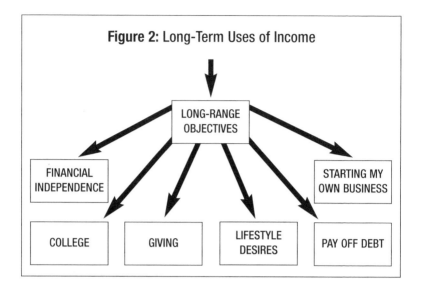

who said his most important long-term goal was to give away at least $1 million toward the fulfillment of the Great Commission. This was the first time I'd considered that people might want to accumulate funds long-term in order to meet a substantial giving goal. This man not only wanted to give the $1 million before retirement; he wanted to give about 15 percent of his total income while he was putting the $1 million aside. He had specific long-term *and* short-term giving objectives.

The long-term goal of "major lifestyle desires" is the area that makes each family unique. The objective could be a different home, a second home, a new car, a particular vacation, or redecorating or remodeling the home. This type of goal finishes the statement "I want to improve my lifestyle by . . ."

Many couples also have a major long-term goal of being completely out of debt, including the debt on their home. We believe it's a worthwhile long-term objective to be totally debt-free.

Lastly, you may want to save in order to start your own business. Your motivation may be to build more flexibility into your schedule, to have more of an influence in the marketplace, or to turn a hobby into an alternative income stream.

Integrated Planning

Figure 3, on the next page, combines the short-term and long-term objectives and outlines a four-step process of financial planning.

Step 1: Summarize your present situation

Step 2: Establish your financial goals

Step 3: Plan to increase your cash flow margin

Step 4: Control your cash flow

If you know where you are, where you're going, and the steps to get there, you will have made a major step toward being a planner rather than a responder, being proactive rather than reactive.

As you review the diagram, you can see the truths we mentioned earlier. Today's decisions determine destiny. There are no independent financial decisions. If you choose to use financial resources in any one area, you've chosen not to use those resources in the other areas.

This means that if you set aside money for college education or financial independence, you no longer have that money available to spend on giving, lifestyle desires, debt repayment, and the like. Similarly, if you decide to spend money on lifestyle desires, you no longer have those resources available for any other short-term or long-term goals.

Another truth implied in the diagram is this: The more long-term your perspective, the more likely it is that you'll make a good financial decision now. A friend and close confidant once defined financial maturity as "giving up today's desires for future benefits." If you choose to give up something today in order to save for tomorrow, you probably have made a wise financial decision.

Perhaps the most dramatic example of the benefits of long-term thinking is in choosing a husband or wife. Taking a long-term perspective in that decision makes for a better choice than simply

Figure 3: Financial Planning Diagram

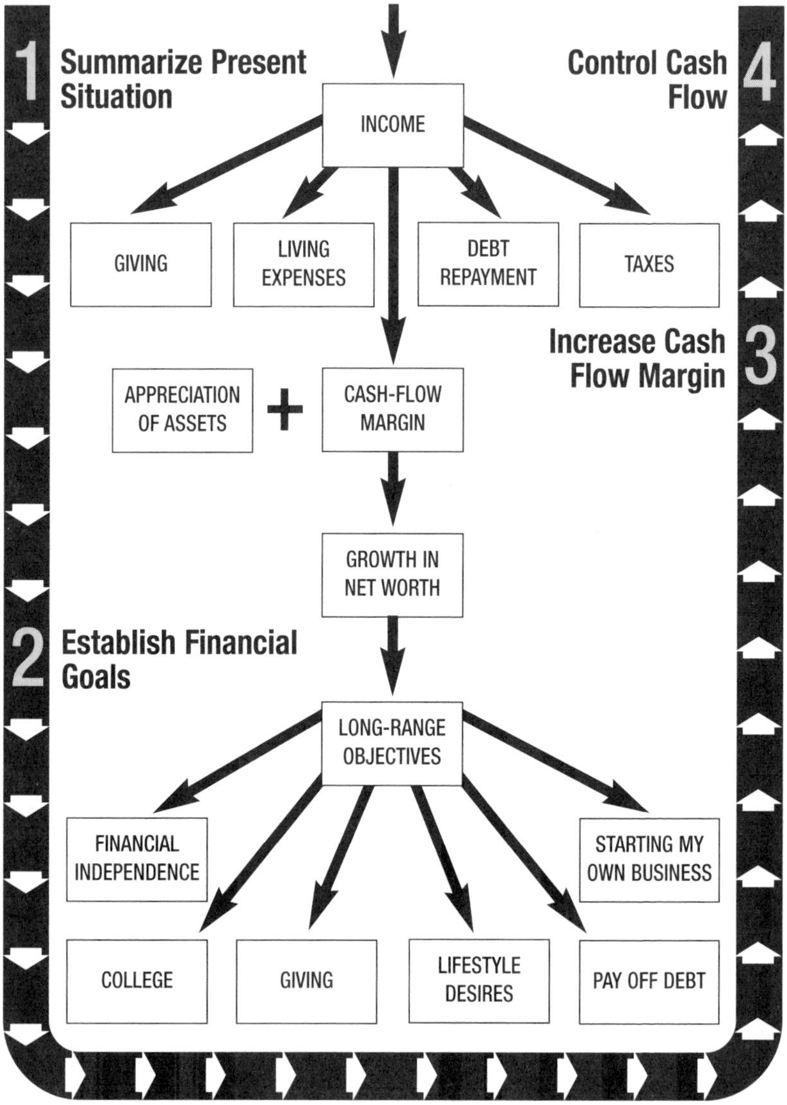

1 Summarize Present Situation

INCOME

GIVING

LIVING EXPENSES

DEBT REPAYMENT

TAXES

APPRECIATION OF ASSETS **+** CASH-FLOW MARGIN

GROWTH IN NET WORTH

2 Establish Financial Goals

LONG-RANGE OBJECTIVES

FINANCIAL INDEPENDENCE

COLLEGE

GIVING

LIFESTYLE DESIRES

PAY OFF DEBT

STARTING MY OWN BUSINESS

Control Cash Flow 4

Increase Cash Flow Margin 3

satisfying a short-term desire. The same principle holds true in financial decisions.

You can also see from this diagram the lifetime nature of financial decisions. We mentioned earlier that three short-term uses of money are consumptive and two are productive. Whenever money is used consumptively, it's gone forever; it can never be used for anything in the future. Once you make a decision to save or spend, you've determined, to some extent, your financial destiny.

In other words, you can't have everything you want when you want it.

But when *can* you have it?

Many questions about financial planning relate to the sequence of when steps should be taken. As the Sequential Accumulation Strategy chart (Figure 4) shows on the following page, we recommend you complete certain steps, such as paying off credit card debt, before other steps, such as investing.

Where Are You Going?

A key to success is knowing where you're going in life and how to get there. But the financial goals we've talked about so far aren't what we're really trying to accomplish in life. Goals like the following better reflect the real desires of our hearts:

Security	Obedience to God
Properly trained children	Personal growth
Peace	Rest and relaxation
Contentment	Self-worth
Flexibility	Acceptance
Comfort	Sense of belonging

Money, then, is one of the resources you use to fulfill the desires you have. Success is knowing what God would have you be and do, and how to achieve that—so that when you stand before Him, you may hear Him say, *"Well done, good and faithful servant!"* (Matthew 25:23).

Figure 4: Sequential Accumulation Strategy

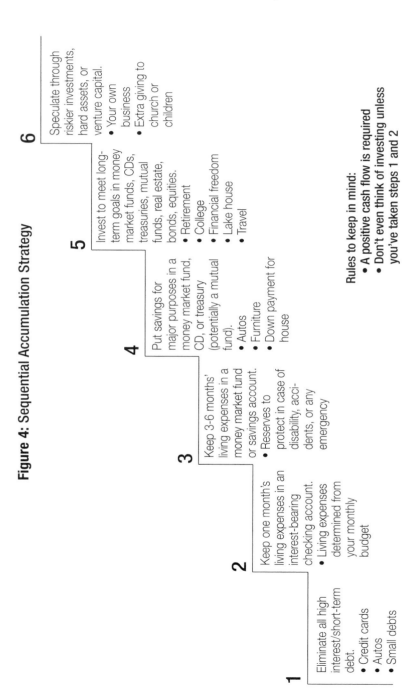

1
Eliminate all high interest/short-term debt.
• Credit cards
• Autos
• Small debts

2
Keep one month's living expenses in an interest-bearing checking account.
• Living expenses determined from your monthly budget

3
Keep 3-6 months' living expenses in a money market fund or savings account.
• Reserves to protect in case of disability, accidents, or any emergency

4
Put savings for major purposes in a money market fund, CD, or treasury (potentially a mutual fund).
• Autos
• Furniture
• Down payment for house

5
Invest to meet long-term goals in money market funds, CDs, treasuries, mutual funds, real estate, bonds, equities.
• Retirement
• College
• Financial freedom
• Lake house
• Travel

6
Speculate through riskier investments, hard assets, or venture capital.
• Your own business
• Extra giving to church or children

Rules to keep in mind:
• A positive cash flow is required
• Don't even think of investing unless you've taken steps 1 and 2

When money becomes your focus, you're doomed to disappointment. Money is merely a resource. It was never intended by the Creator to be anything more than that. That's one of the most important financial principles any parent can model.

Though walking—setting the example—is louder than talking, wise parents combine both. The next chapter will give you some idea of what's best to tell your children about financial matters.

Talking the Talk

From a Child's Perspective:

MOTHER: "Why on earth did you swallow the money I gave you?"

JUNIOR: "You said it was my lunch money."

Beauty is skin deep. But how rich you are can last a long time.
—CHRISTINE, AGE 9

Biblical Principles:

Choose my instruction instead of silver, knowledge rather than choice gold, for wisdom is more precious than rubies, and nothing you desire can compare with her.—PROVERBS 8:10-11

Whoever can be trusted with very little can also be trusted with much, and whoever is dishonest with very little will also be dishonest with much. So if you have not been trustworthy in handling worldly wealth, who will trust you with true riches?—LUKE 16:10-11

In our grandparents' generation, it was taboo to talk about sex and money. Both are still tough subjects for many families today.

How odd that parents hesitate to teach about these two

powerful motivators—factors capable of enhancing or ruining their children's lives.

Do you think you can't teach your kids about sex and money? If you don't, the media, slick marketers, credit card companies, and ill-informed peers will. Swallow your pride, ignore your embarrassment, get the facts, and give them to your kids. It's your job—and you clearly take it seriously, or you wouldn't be reading this.

We'll focus on only one of these topics in this chapter (though a discussion about sex might perk up your interest in this book!).

"We Never Discussed Money"

Forbes magazine published an article about how the well-known Kennedy family fared with its wealth. The patriarch, Joseph Kennedy, was an adept businessman. Some may argue about how ethical some of his practices were, but Joe Kennedy was successful in controlling a chain of movie houses, a movie studio, prime real estate in various cities, and liquor distribution companies.

Yet none of his nine children and almost none of his 29 grandchildren has shown any interest or skill in business or managing money. The Kennedy clan is good at *spending* the money; some have estimated its dwindling fortune may not last past the next generation.

The *Forbes* article identified a possible culprit for the lack of business acumen in the descendents:

> Blame Joseph P. himself, the founding father of the fortune.
> Many families don't believe in talking about business at the
> dinner table. Joseph Kennedy took that one step further.
> He didn't believe in talking business to his family at all.
> "We never discussed money in the house because, well,
> money isn't important," old Joe told one of his son Jack's
> biographers.[1]

That's a surprising attitude from someone who devoted his life to earning money. Some people think they earn too much to talk to their families about finances; others think they earn too little to make it a topic of conversation. As we mentioned in the last chapter, walking the walk is more important than talking the talk. More is caught than taught. But imagine the powerful influence you can have if you do both. If you walk *and* talk, you give your kids an excellent chance to be financially competent.

What do we mean by "talking the talk"? As you go about your day-to-day business, speak the right words. In this chapter we'll look at how to do that in the following ways:

- Go beyond meaningless, even harmful, clichés.
- Speak the truth in love.
- Share with your kids the level of financial assistance you plan to give them.
- Put financial and economic terms in everyday language.
- Discuss certain financial details while keeping others confidential.

Don't Be So Cliché!

As a child, did you ever suspect all parents went to the same parenting school?

It seemed they used the same phrases. For example, you probably heard some form of this familiar refrain: "Clean your plate. Starving kids on the other side of the world would love to eat that broccoli."

You suspected that such sayings contained a bit of truth, but you questioned them. If you were a smart aleck, you may have responded to the broccoli admonition with, "Well, why don't we just send this broccoli to those kids and everyone will be happy?"

The alleged parental wisdom found in knee-jerk clichés doesn't work. Did the "starving kids" ploy ever motivate you? Probably not.

When parents use these phrases, kids respond by leaning back their heads, cocking them slightly to the side, making a face, and then—here it comes—rolling their eyes.

You know now, of course, that there's no parenting school. It's genetic coding! Even when you try to avoid sounding like your parents, those genes kick in. The DNA encoding sends instructions to your brain and you spout the same clichés you heard from your parents. Your hand flies to your mouth, but it's too late. You sound just like your mother.

Parents often suffer this malady when it comes to money matters. They fling clichés and think they've given valuable instructions. They respond to whining in the Wal-Mart toy department with something like, "Do you think I'm made of money?"

Poof! The teachable moment vanishes. Whether the parents see it or not, their kids' eyes are rolling.

Here's our Top Ten list of ways to waste your breath when talking about money:

Top Ten Useless Things
Parents Say to Their Kids about Money

10. You're penny wise and pound foolish.
9. That money is burning a hole in your pocket.
8. When you're bringing home the bacon, you can buy all the (fill in the blank) you want.
7. We can't afford that; I don't have two nickels to rub together.
6. You don't know the value of a dollar.
5. What do you think I am, a bank?
4. Don't spend it all in one place.
3. Save for a rainy day.
2. A penny saved is a penny earned.

And the number one useless thing parents say to kids about money (drum roll, please) . . .

1. Money doesn't grow on trees.

Okay, you don't have to confess how many of these you've said. Let's just say you can do better.

Some of these quotes no longer have meaning, and some provide only a partial truth. There's nothing wrong with saying "Money doesn't grow on trees." If you say it, don't assume you've transferred valuable, behavior-changing instruction.

Let's look more closely at the top three.

"Save for a rainy day." This one has lost its meaning to the younger generation. In the olden days, most kids' activities were outside. A rainy day meant nothing to do. Having some savings might mean a chance to brighten the day with ice cream or a movie.

Today, kids rarely play outside. They think, *If it rains, so what? I get to spend more time on the computer or watching videos or TV or going to the mall, just like I do on sunny days.*

Instead of, "Save for a rainy day," perhaps we should just say, "Be prepared for surprises. Keep an emergency fund."

"A penny saved is a penny earned." This isn't the whole truth. As we'll learn from our activities with compounding and the opportunity cost of spending money now, a penny saved today results in multiple pennies in the future. A penny spent today takes a dime from tomorrow.

Inflation has wreaked havoc on Benjamin Franklin's aphorism. Remember when you could buy a piece of gum for a penny? A penny buys nothing anymore. Pennies don't motivate kids. Next time you're tempted to use this saying, try something like, "A dollar saved means many dollars later."

"Money doesn't grow on trees." Have your children said it did? They never saw money on a tree. They never noticed "money buds" in spring. They never saw dollar bills change color in the fall. While they're trying to picture such strange vegetation, they miss the point you're trying to make about how money should be spent wisely because it's not just waiting to be "picked."

To older kids, this obvious fact sounds like condescension. It builds up resistance to what you're trying to teach.

Rather than relying on this old standby, you might switch it around to say, "Money can grow like a tree." Now you're planting a vision of truth, saying something constructive.

You could carry the analogy further. Money can be used as a tree is used; consumed, it provides a short-term benefit, but it's gone forever. That's what happens when you spend your money on candy and the trinkets in 50-cent vending machines. Or it can be used to "build" a fund for something more lasting, like a car or house. Or, just as a tree's acorns or roots or seedlings can start a whole forest, investing can yield more and more "trees"—even for future generations.

Speak Gold Nuggets of Truth in Love

Rather than repeating clichés, speak biblical truths. When you teach the wisdom found in God's inspired Word, you lay a solid foundation for your kids.

Try quoting Bible verses or memorable portions of Bible verses. This is what you want your kids to remember you saying. If they ask what your new phraseology means, point them to the whole Bible passage to see the context.

Memorize an entire passage yourself and then teach it to your kids. In this way you'll be showing them that you believe, as Paul instructed Timothy, that *"All Scripture is God-breathed and is useful for teaching, rebuking, correcting and training in righteousness"* (2 Timothy 3:16).

Remember what we said in Chapter 1 about integrating God's truth "as you go"? Talk about His biblical principles—nuggets of truth—when you drive along the road, when you sit at home, when you're tucking your children in at night. Here are some examples to get you started.

Gold Nugget of Truth	Complete Bible Reference	Desired Attribute; Teaching Opportunity
Be a cheerful giver.	*"Each man should give what he has decided in his heart to give, not reluctantly or under compulsion, for God loves a cheerful giver."* 2 Corinthians 9:7	Generous giver. Remind kids when they are giving to do so joyfully. Use when they are reluctant to share or give to others.
Don't rob God.	*"Will a man rob God? Yet you rob me. But you ask, 'How do we rob you?' In tithes and offerings. You are under a curse —the whole nation of you— because you are robbing me. Bring the whole tithe into the storehouse."* Malachi 3:8-10	Generous giver. Use when your child wants to spend rather than give, or when your child wants to take money out of his giving envelope (see Chapter 4).
Consider the ant and be wise.	*"Go to the ant, you sluggard; consider its ways and be wise! It has no commander, no overseer or ruler, yet it stores its provisions in summer and gathers its food at harvest."* Proverbs 6:6-8	Savvy saver. Study the ways of the ants when your child is wanting to buy cheap trinkets instead of saving for something more substantial.
Shrewd as a snake, innocent as a dove.	*"I am sending you out like sheep among wolves. Therefore be as shrewd as snakes and as innocent as doves."* Matthew 10:16	Sharp shopper. Use when your child is being swayed by misleading advertising or claims.

Gold Nugget of Truth	Complete Bible Reference	Desired Attribute; Teaching Opportunity
Lay up treasure for yourselves.	*"Command them to do good, to be rich in good deeds, and to be generous and willing to share. In this way they will lay up treasure for themselves as a firm foundation for the coming age, so that they may take hold of the life that is truly life."* 1 Timothy 6:18-19	Generous giver. Use to challenge your child to give above and beyond her typical giving, to encourage her to share with others in need.
The borrower is slave to the lender.	*"The rich rule over the poor, and the borrower is servant to the lender."* Proverbs 22:7	Sharp shopper. Use when discussing the drawbacks to credit cards and borrowing from others.
Count the cost.	*"Suppose one of you wants to build a tower. Will he not first sit down and estimate the cost to see if he has enough money to complete it?"* Luke 14:28	Prudent planner. Calculate the cost of an impulse purchase—such as a candy bar at a convenience store, compared to buying a 12-pack of bars in advance at a discount store.
Love of money is the root of all kinds of evil.	*"For the love of money is a root of all kinds of evil. Some people, eager for money, have wandered from the faith and pierced themselves with many griefs."* 1 Timothy 6:10	Generous giver. Sharp shopper. Savvy saver. Prudent planner. Use when your child is showing tendencies to hoard or an unwillingness to share.

Gold Nugget of Truth	Complete Bible Reference	Desired Attribute; Teaching Opportunity
You will reap what you sow.	*"Do not be deceived: God cannot be mocked. A man reaps what he sows."* Galatians 6:7	Intelligent investor. Use to encourage patience and long-term perspective in saving and investing.
Don't bury your treasure.	*"'So I was afraid and went out and hid your talent in the ground. See, here is what belongs to you.' His master replied, 'You wicked, lazy servant! So you knew that I harvest where I have not sown and gather where I have not scattered seed? Well then, you should have put my money on deposit with the bankers, so that when I returned I would have received it back with interest.'"* Matthew 25:25-27	Intelligent investor. Use when your child is reluctant to take a risk with her money to start a business, begin a new job, save in a banking account, or invest.
Talk leads to poverty.	*"All hard work brings a profit, but mere talk leads only to poverty."* Proverbs 14:23	Willing worker. Use when your child says he's going to do something "in a minute," but is slow about getting around to it.
If you don't work, you don't eat.	*"For even when we were with you, we gave you this rule: 'If a man will not work, he shall not eat.'"* 2 Thessalonians 3:10	Willing worker. Use when your child is negligent in her chores or is showing a lack of initiative.

Speak these "in love." Use them to teach, not just to imply, "I told you so," or to get your kids to be quiet when they're whining. The Word of God will accomplish its purpose. *"So is my word that goes out from my mouth: It will not return to me empty, but will accomplish what I desire and achieve the purpose for which I sent it"* (Isaiah 55:11).

Sharing with Your Kids Your Level of Financial Assistance

When you make decisions and communicate them effectively to children, much of the reason for conflict disappears. Expectations and reality become one. Conflict occurs more easily when reality doesn't meet expectations. This is especially true with family finances.

For example, if a child expects a new car at age 16 but the parents never planned that, at age 16 the child is likely to be disappointed, hurt, or angry—regardless of what his parents give him for his birthday.

Or maybe the child expects her parents to buy all her clothes through high school; at age 16 she finds out they had no plans to buy her clothes once she was old enough to work. Again, expectations and reality don't agree. The result is "generation gap" at best, open rebellion at worst.

Talking with children about their expectations won't prevent every miscommunication, but it's a big step. It gives them the security of knowing where the boundaries are and what they should be prepared for. Without this communication, children may expect you to support them in the lifestyle promoted by advertisements and movies. The greater the difference between expectation and reality, the greater the pain for all involved.

In addition to establishing boundaries, communicating your plans gives parents and children a familiar track to run on for many years. For example, we (the Blues) have told our children what financial assistance they can expect from us after they're married. This enables all of us to better map our own financial lives.

Through prayer and planning, we've predetermined what our children can expect of us—instead of waiting for them to tell us what they expect. That's what a formal training plan is all about.

Speak the Language of Finance and Economics

Do you ever wonder why it seems the children of wealthy parents often become wealthy themselves? Some of the effect may be explained by the wealthy affording better education opportunities, health care, and cultural involvement. In our opinion, it's the financial examples and modeling that make the most significant impressions on kids.

It's always gratifying to have your opinion backed up by academic research. A study by two economics professors concluded that wealthy parents help their kids by passing along good financial habits: "Children's savings propensities are determined by mimicking their parents' behavior."[2]

Although many view the United States as a land of opportunity, an article in *The Wall Street Journal* summarized recent research indicating that the rich-to-poor gap is widening. However, the studies found that parents can confer an edge to their kids. Bhashkar Mazumder, a Federal Reserve Bank of Chicago economist, concluded, "The apple falls even closer to the tree than we thought."[3]

Robert Kiyosaki, author of *Rich Dad, Poor Dad: What the Rich Teach Their Kids about Money That the Poor and Middle Class Do Not* (Warner Business Books, 2000), said the most important difference between his "poor" dad (his father, a school superintendent) and his "rich dad" (his mentor and best friend's father, a successful businessman and investor) was the words they used. Rich people used "rich" words and poor people used "poor" words.

His rich dad spoke the language of commerce. He spoke of investing in real estate, building businesses, and acquiring assets. He said that school is important but financial literacy is more important. His "poor," educated dad knew the language of academia, but never bothered to learn how money worked. Though he earned a fairly significant salary, he lived from paycheck to paycheck.

What a shame it would be if your kids earned good grades in school but were financially illiterate. But it happens over and over. In America, where people are "more educated" than ever, more and more of them have filed for bankruptcy during recent years—even during relatively healthy economic times!

In addition to the activities we've provided and the example you're providing, you must use financial topics and information in your conversations. You may not be a CPA or an investment professional, but you've learned quite a bit from the School of Hard Knocks. Be open about financial mistakes you may have made. Also share your good decisions, such as why you refinanced your mortgage when interest rates dropped.

Let's say that every day, driving your daughter home from school, you ask the same old question: "How was school today?" Every day you hear the same old response: "Fine."

Instead, throw out a question as you pass a nice house: "How do you think the people in that house earned their money?" Your daughter may have some interesting responses. You don't have to know the answer, but you can discuss how they likely worked hard in school to learn a profession or began a business or saved their money for many years.

When newspaper headlines talk about rising interest rates, help your kids see the effects on various groups. For example, you could explain that people who are saving money will like it because they'll earn more on their savings accounts or certificates of deposit. People borrowing money won't like it because they may have to pay more interest. Businesses that have to pay more interest on loans may earn less or raise prices to keep earning the same money.

Instead of arguing about the music your children want to listen to on road trips, think about a financial matter to discuss. We (Ron and Judy) remember using a long road trip to Disney World as a teachable "moment." We safeguarded some of our kids' savings instead of depositing the money in a bank, gave them an "interest credit" in cash, and brought this with us. After we explained, they asked, "What can we do with it?"

We told them they could spend it on our trip—in addition to the spending money they'd already brought—or keep it as savings to earn even more interest. They all decided to put it back when they understood how much interest can accumulate. (You'll find more interest-related activities in Chapter 8 of this book.)

You can use your occupation as a conversation starter, too. If you're an employee of a company or a business owner, explain why you think sales were up this month. Let your kids know your insights about the effect of a new advertising campaign, better trained employees, or the introduction of new products or services. Talk to them about your company's niche market or what's unique about its customer service.

You may be surprised at how much financial information your kids have heard but don't really understand. Recently, I (Jeremy) was driving and listening to the news about Social Security. I asked my daughters if they knew what that was. They said their grand-parents seemed very interested in it. My girls thought it was some-thing that companies gave to older people. They also knew it had been in the news a lot.

I was surprised at how much they'd absorbed at their ages—10 and 12 at the time—even if they were off a bit in who provided it. I explained how taxes were collected from people like me to pro-vide for the elderly and disabled. They were shocked to learn that the government doesn't keep an account stored away for me with my contributions in it. They raised their eyebrows when I explained they and their peers would be paying taxes to provide for me and my peers in our old age.

How old will kids be before someone teaches this in a class-room? Will they learn it in high school? College?

This was no hour-long lecture, just a brief discussion. But it broadened their awareness on an important issue. Now I can refer back to this conversation when talking about the importance of saving and investing because Social Security may not exist for them. I can use the Monopoly game and "Cashflow for Kids" activity (see Chapter 10) to explain why investment income and rental income are beneficial for tax purposes, since you don't have to pay Social Security tax on that income as you do on a salary. That's a tremendous financial fact most adults haven't grasped.

Don't assume these conversations are too difficult for your kids. If they can master downloading music from the Internet to an iPod, and if they can operate functions on your cell phone that you don't know about, they can understand that the Dow Jones report they hear on the radio refers to how the stock market closed today.

What to Say (and Not Say) about More Sensitive Financial Matters

We've emphasized the value of talking about money and related topics, but your parenting instincts tell you not to disclose everything. We agree. Your kids may not be ready for all your personal financial details.

Why are you guarded with your kids about your weight, age, or other personal details? Because you suspect the more precocious kid of your litter might share it in public at the most inopportune time and embarrass you.

Most parents don't volunteer confidential financial information. But what if your children ask? If they're likely to ask how much you earn or how much your house cost, you and your spouse (if you have one) should decide in advance how to answer.

We (Ron and Judy) chose to answer the questions directly. We believed answering our kids' questions about money took away the mystery and reduced their curiosity. We know this approach isn't common, but we wanted to maintain open communication with our kids and let them know there was nothing they couldn't ask.

On the other hand, I (Jeremy) have chosen to answer certain

questions with few specifics. Living in a small town and having to maintain strict confidentiality with my clients, I don't want to take the risk of my children telling friends how much savings we have or how much we give. Some things are private and not their business. Whatever approach you take, consider your decision carefully.

Here are a few other reasons you may not want to share details about your finances:

- Your kids may think you're far wealthier than you are. To them, $50,000 in a retirement plan will sound like a fortune because they can't appreciate the cost of living.
- Your kids may lose some motivation. Knowing how much is in their college fund at age 12 or how much their grandparents set aside in a trust fund may give your kids the wrong impression about their work and responsibilities.
- Kids do not need to be burdened with keeping secrets.
- Kids need to learn the importance of maintaining confidentiality of their own financial information.

Still, we suggest you share other important elements of your financial picture. If you decide not to reveal the exact amount of your tithes and offerings, you may want to talk generally about your giving and how you arrive at the amount. You might not show your 13-year-old your will, but he needs to know that you've made plans in the event of your death. (You *have* prepared that will, right?)

Guidelines for Disclosing Personal Financial Information to Your Kids

As your kids become older teenagers, you may choose to share more information. For example, they need to know where wills, life insurance policies, and other important documents are kept. If you and your spouse die in a car wreck on your monthly date night, older kids can be invaluable in helping manage the affairs of the family and in guiding others, such as executors and guardians.

Details Requiring Parental Discretion and Judgment in Sharing with Your Kids	Information Your Kids Should Know
The amount in your retirement plan	The fact that you're saving for retirement and general details (how it's deducted from a paycheck, that you're investing in the stock market, etc.).
The total death benefit of life insurance policies	You have life insurance and have made plans to provide for them in case you die earlier than expected.
Your salary	What you like about your job; what benefits come with your job; a relative range of salary— for example, your education allows you to earn more than a manager of a fast-food restaurant, but less than a doctor; when you get raises or bonuses so everyone can celebrate.
Amount kept in trust funds for your kids	Some plans have been made to help with, but not entirely provide for, their future.
The first and second choices of guardians	Not only have you made plans to provide for them financially, but you've made arrangements for their care with others you trust.
The net worth of your parents (their grandparents) and the amount of an inheritance	Let your parents lead the way in how much to share.

Details Requiring Parental Discretion and Judgment in Sharing with Your Kids	Information Your Kids Should Know
All your past financial dirty laundry: how many times you bounced a check, the blemishes on your credit report, or how much money you wasted in college	Sharing certain failures at appropriate times can be helpful in teaching kids. Discuss the investment you bought on impulse and lost money on. Talk about what you learned. Have a good laugh about the old clunker car you bought that spent more time in the shop than on the road. Keep it light and for the purpose of making a point.
The details of your will	You've made plans for your family and possessions in the unlikely event of a premature death.
The amount in the college fund	You've made plans to assist with paying for college; you've begun investing it wisely.

The Best Activity to Pull It All Together

From a Child's Perspective:
Instead of going to the candy store or buying junk, you can save money and spend it on something you really want like toys and other stuff.—JON, AGE 9

I have been saving money, but I can't spend any because my parents are using my piggybank for a doorstop.—ASHTON, AGE 6

Biblical Principles:
Blessed is the man who perseveres under trial, because when he has stood the test, he will receive the crown of life that God has promised to those who love him.—JAMES 1:12

Commit to the LORD whatever you do, and your plans will succeed.
—PROVERBS 16:3

What causes fights and quarrels among you? Don't they come from your desires that battle within you? You want something but don't get it. You kill and covet, but you cannot have what you want. You quarrel and fight. You do not have, because you do not ask God.

When you ask, you do not receive, because you ask with wrong motives, that you may spend what you get on your pleasures.
—JAMES 4:1-3

We (Judy and Ron) presented an envelope training system as the centerpiece of our 1992 book, *Raising Money-Smart Kids*. Since that time, we've received overwhelmingly positive feedback from parents—and even children. We're always thankful to have young adults approach us to tell how their "envelope" experience helped them.

The concept is simple, but the results are powerful. We'll go into detail during this chapter, but here's the essence of the system.

You as parents fund with cash certain categories for your kids, such as clothes. Give kids the cash amount you've budgeted for them to put in specific envelopes. Let them have the control and responsibility over spending the envelope amounts. Categories may include entertainment and clothes. Over time, you may expand to school supplies, gifts for others, or music lessons.

Some may consider this an allowance. In reality, you're turning over certain areas of the family budget—items you'd be paying for—to your child, to develop his or her financial skills.

The envelope system establishes boundaries, reveals clearly where you stand, empowers your child, and actually frees him or her. This system opens the lines of communication so that you and your child are on the same side of the fence.

In researching and preparing for this book, I (Jeremy) tried this idea in our family. We saw instant, positive results with our girls in the area of clothing.

Previously, a battle had ensued every time my wife and daughters went shopping. Our kids never knew exactly how much we were planning to spend on their clothes. They had no incentive to find the best deal. They begged, pleaded, whined, compared, complained, cajoled, manipulated, argued, and reasoned their way to our wallet and purse. They figured out what buttons to push in an attempt to get what they wanted. It was a tug-of-war; they tugged, and we pulled back.

We knew this approach wasn't working, so we decided to take a different one. After looking at our family budget and what we'd spent last year on clothes, we began funding the girls' "clothing" envelope. We simply put the amount we were planning to spend anyway in their envelopes. We let them decide what to spend (retaining the right to veto purchases based on modesty, appropriateness, or other compelling reasons).

In less than a year, our kids became wiser shoppers and better planners. They made a list of their clothing needs at the beginning of the quarter. Then, with list in hand, they went shopping with my wife.

When we praise our children for shopping wisely, it brings a smile to their faces. We're smiling, too, because we're on their team —giving advice instead of fighting so many battles!

We don't claim to have invented the idea of putting money in a container in order to control spending. The simplest, yet most effective, approach to managing money may have been Grandma's cookie jar.

That's right! Grandma's system was simply to put income received into the jar and to take money out as needs occurred. When the jar was empty, that signaled the end of spending. No credit, no robbing Peter to pay Paul, no payday check advances.

Many parents used that system. As household management became more complex, they gave up the cookie jar and switched to envelopes.

Cookie jars and envelopes both demonstrate a basic, but profound, financial planning principle: The outgo can never be greater than the inflow. The cookie jar is not a bottomless pit; when the jar is empty, you're done spending.

In training our children, we've used multiple "cookie jars," which are merely letter-sized envelopes with a label on the outside indicating how the cash in the envelope is to be used. These envelopes are kept in a file box or recipe box. The beauty of the envelopes is that the spending can never be greater than the amount originally put in.

Two elements are necessary in any budget, whether it's for family, business, or government. Those elements are a *plan* for spending and a *system of controls* to ensure that the spending is never greater than the plan allows.

Too many of us, however, behave as if these two elements were no longer relevant or necessary. Credit allows us to live in the short term, as if there were no bottom to the cookie jar and no limit to our spending.

Deficit spending, at every level, has made any budgeting plan almost irrelevant, because financing always seems available to go beyond what was planned. A crisis surfaces only when all sources of credit have dried up, and a lifestyle has been established far beyond the ability to repay. At this point, the options are so devastating that many couples end up in severe conflict. This results in stress and division, sometimes even divorce or personal bankruptcy.

I (Ron) have counseled many godly families who were in desperate financial conditions because they had no plan for spending. The opportunity to fund their needs and greeds by using credit cards had enabled them to overspend year after year.

When they ran out of credit, they had to make some tough decisions. Houses and cars had to be sold, children had to be taken out of private schools, clothing budgets had to be readjusted, and standards of living had to undergo dramatic reduction in order for these families to survive.

Had they followed the basics of the cookie jar or envelope system, they never would have gotten into such poor financial shape. Did these people *plan to fail*? No, they merely *failed to plan*—and failed to choose to live within a plan.

They found that debt is no man's friend; it will always make you a slave.

The Mechanics of Our Envelope System

The system we used with our (Ron and Judy's) children was very simple. We gave each child, beginning at about age eight, a recipe file box containing five letter-sized envelopes: a Tithe envelope, a Save envelope, a Spend envelope, a Gifts envelope, and a Clothes envelope.

The Spend envelope contained money that could be used in any way they chose. The Gift envelope was the amount allocated for buying gifts at Christmas, birthdays, and other special occasions for friends and relatives. The Clothes amount was used to purchase *all* their clothes.

They were given a monthly allowance, in cash, to place in each of the envelopes according to a preset plan. The amount set for each envelope came from an annual planning session that Judy and I had. We discussed the allowance amounts for each of the five categories, based on what our kids were required to pay for; then we gave them one-twelfth of that amount each month in a lump sum.

As they earned money or received gift money during the year, they deposited it in at least three envelopes, and sometimes all five envelopes. When they were beginning to learn about the system, they were required to put 10 percent into the Tithe envelope and 10 percent into the Save envelope. The balance could go into the Spend, Gift, and Clothes envelopes.

As they got older and understood the purpose of the system, our kids were given the freedom to divide the money as they saw fit. We tried to help them see the value and benefit of giving and saving. When they chose for themselves, they enjoyed the experience of decision making.

Each family has to decide what children will be responsible for in the various categories. But the most important thing is not *what* children are responsible for buying, but how they handle the responsibility of managing the money. They need to learn that when the money is gone, there is no more. They must learn to live within the designated amount.

If you want your kids to buy their own sports equipment, for instance, that's great. Allocate enough money to the "clothes" envelope so that they can cover those expenses, then require them to make the purchase.

Children may make the mistake of poor allocation. For example, if you've chosen to give your children a lump sum for an entire season of clothing, one child may spend all his money in October for fall clothes and, consequently, have no money left to buy the desperately needed winter coat.

There are several ways to deal with this challenge. First, you may decide *not* to make them responsible for what you consider to be the "necessities"—winter coats, snow boots, Sunday shoes, haircuts, school lunches, and so forth. *You* provide the money for those things. Or, second, you can let them do without. Third, they can live with the consequences of wearing last year's coat or boots. Fourth, you can have them earn the extra money needed for the purchase.

You can come up with other creative alternatives. The point is that children should have responsibility for certain budget items, and they must learn to allocate properly within those budget categories.

For a larger purchase, such as a bicycle, tennis racquet, or seasonal wardrobe, children may need several weeks or months before they accumulate enough to make the transaction. But when they've saved enough, they can take the envelope with them and pay for the item with cash.

We allowed our children to borrow from envelope to envelope, except for the Tithe and Save categories. They needed to feel responsible for the management of the money, so we allowed them quite a bit of flexibility in how they spent it.

Your child's Save envelope accumulates money that he or she may spend on a specific item or deposit periodically in a savings account. As we'll discuss in the compounding activities, you can show your child how the interest causes that account to "grow" without his or her having to expend any physical or mental energy.

Principles and Practices

Children can begin to manage money at early ages. By age eight or nine, many kids can handle all five envelopes, planning for and buying all their clothes and all the gifts they need. The significant purchases—such as clothes and gifts—will require the greatest amount of discretion and provide the greatest value in training, right on through the college years.

When children reach adolescence they may choose to have more envelopes, and that's okay. Still, we didn't encourage our children to have more than six or seven envelopes until they reached college age. The system needs to be simple to work most effectively.

We've included some completed sample budgets for a 13-year-old boy (Charts 1, 2, 3, 4) to help you determine the allowance per budget category. These are followed by budget worksheet forms you can use with your own children. The amount per category will vary by age, activities, family income, and lifestyle choices; the amounts included may be high or low for your family, and are shown only as examples of working through the numbers.

Every child is unique and will have different financial requirements. Some will spend more time participating in sports or taking music lessons than others. So, the funding amounts should vary accordingly. As children reach the teen years, they may have earnings they can use to meet some of the budget categories.

CHART 1
Budget Worksheet: Clothes
(Sample for 13-year-old boy)

I. Clothes	Estimated Annual Amount (1)
A. Seasonal wardrobe	
1. Fall	$ 100
2. Winter	$ 150
3. Spring	$ 100
4. Summer	$ 75
B. Underwear and socks	$ 30
C. Shoes	
1. Dress	$ 100
2. Everyday	$ 135
3. Sports	$ 75
D. Coats	
1. Winter	$ 120
2. Spring	$ 75
E. Athletic clothes and equipment	$ 200
F. Accessories (ties, belts, jewelry)	$ 40

CHART 1 (cont.)

G. Other (band uniforms, etc.) $ __0__
                                        $ __0__
                                        $ __0__
                                        $ __0__
                                        $ __0__

Annual total $1,200 (2)

Monthly amount needed
(annual total divided by 12) $ 100 (3)

Subtract amount provided
by allowance $ (80) (4)

Amount to come from earnings
and other sources $ _20_ (5)

1. Estimate annual amount for each category.
2. Add the amounts in all categories to get an annual total.
3. Divide the annual total (2) by 12 to get monthly amount.
4. Subtract the amount the parents will provide as a monthly allowance.
5. The monthly amount (3) less the allowance amount (4) results in the amount that must be provided from earnings, gifts, and other sources.

CHART 2
Budget Worksheet: Spend
(Sample for 13-year-old boy)

II. Spend	Estimated Annual Amount (1)
A. Food and snacks (school lunches, etc.)	$ <u>480</u>
B. Entertainment (movies, sports, etc.)	$ <u>240</u>
C. Hobbies	$ <u>84</u>
D. CDs/DVDs/music and video downloads	$ <u>60</u>
E. Jewelry	$ <u>0</u>
F. Personal grooming (haircuts, etc.)	$ <u>48</u>
G. Reading material (books, magazines)	$ <u>84</u>
H. School supplies	$ <u>144</u>

CHART 2 (cont.)

I. Auto
    1. Insurance $ __0
    2. Gas, oil, maintenance $ __0
    3. Repairs $ __0
    4. Tires $ __0

Annual total $1,140 (2)

Monthly amount needed
(annual total divided by 12) $ _95_ (3)

Subtract amount provided
by allowance $ (65) (4)

Amount to come from earnings
and other sources $ _30_ (5)

1. Estimate annual amount for each category.
2. Add the amounts in all categories to get an annual total.
3. Divide the annual total (2) by 12 to get monthly amount.
4. Subtract the amount the parents will provide as a monthly allowance.
5. The monthly amount (3) less the allowance amount (4) results in the amount that must be provided from earnings, gifts, and other sources.

CHART 3
Budget Worksheet: Gifts
(Sample for 13-year-old boy)

III. Gifts	Estimated Annual Amount (1)		Total (2)
	Family	Friends	
A. Christmas	$ 100	$ 20	$ 120
B. Birthdays	$ 100	$ 20	$ 120
C. Anniversaries	$ 10	$ 0	$ 10
D. Mother's/Father's Day	$ 20	$ 0	$ 20
E. Special Occasions			
1. Graduations	$ 10	$ 0	$ 10
2. Weddings	$ 0	$ 0	$ 0
3. Valentine's Day	$ 10	$ 10	$ 20
4. Easter	$ 0	$ 0	$ 0
5. Other	$ 0	$ 0	$ 0

CHART 3 (cont.)

F. Other	$ __0	$ __0	$ __0
Annual total	$ 250	$ _50	$ 300

Monthly amount needed
(annual total divided by 12) $ _25 (3)

Subtract amount provided by allowance $ (15) (4)

Amount to come from earnings
and other sources $ _10 (5)

1. Estimate annual amount for each category.
2. Add the amounts in all categories to get an annual total.
3. Divide the annual total (2) by 12 to get monthly amount.
4. Subtract the amount the parents will provide as a monthly allowance.
5. The monthly amount (3) less the allowance amount (4) results in the amount that must be provided from earnings, gifts, and other sources.

CHART 4
Monthly Plan
(Sample for 13-year-old boy)

	Monthly Amount Needed	Allowance	Earnings, Etc.
Clothes (1)	$ 100	$ 80	$ 20
Spend	$ 85	$ 65	$ 20
Gifts	$ 25	$ 15	$ 10
Total (2)	$ 210	$ 160	$ 50
Save (10 percent of total) (2)	$ 21	$ 16	$ 5
Tithe (10 percent of total) (2)	$ 21	$ 16	$ 5
Total monthly plan (2)	$ 252	$ 192	$ 60

1. Copy totals from appropriate budget worksheets for "monthly amount needed" [worksheet line (3)], "allowance" [worksheet line (4)], and "earnings, etc." [worksheet line (5)].
2. Add to get total for each category.
3. Multiply (2) by 10 percent (or another desired percentage).
4. Multiply (2) by 10 percent (or another desired percentage).
5. Add the total (2) the save (3), and the tithe (4) amounts to determine the total monthly plan.

CHART 5
Budget Worksheet: Clothes

I. Clothes	**Estimated Annual Amount (1)**
A. Seasonal wardrobe	
1. Fall	$ ____
2. Winter	$ ____
3. Spring	$ ____
4. Summer	$ ____
B. Underwear and socks	$ ____
C. Shoes	
1. Dress	$ ____
2. Everyday	$ ____
3. Sports	$ ____
D. Coats	
1. Winter	$ ____
2. Spring	$ ____
E. Athletic clothes and equipment	$ ____
F. Accessories (ties, belts, jewelry)	$ ____

CHART 5 (cont.)

G. Other (band uniforms, etc.) $ ____

                                            $ ____

                                            $ ____

                                            $ ____

Annual total $ ____ (2)

Monthly amount needed
(annual total divided by 12) $ ____ (3)

Subtract amount provided
by allowance $(____) (4)

Amount to come from earnings
and other sources $ ____ (5)

1. Estimate annual amount for each category.
2. Add the amounts in all categories to get an annual total.
3. Divide the annual total (2) by 12 to get monthly amount.
4. Subtract the amount the parents will provide as a monthly allowance.
5. The monthly amount (3) less the allowance amount (4) results in the amount that must be provided from earnings, gifts, and other sources.

CHART 6
Budget Worksheet: Spend

II. Spend	Estimated Annual Amount (1)
A. Food and snacks (school lunches, etc.)	$ ____
B. Entertainment (movies, sports, etc.)	$ ____
C. Hobbies	$ ____
D. CDs/DVDs/music and video downloads	$ ____
E. Jewelry	$ ____
F. Personal grooming (haircuts, etc.)	$ ____
G. Reading material (books, magazines)	$ ____
H. School supplies	$ ____

CHART 6 (cont.)

I. Auto
    1. Insurance $ _____
    2. Gas, oil, maintenance $ _____
    3. Repairs $ _____
    4. Tires $ _____

Annual total $ _____ (2)

Monthly amount needed
(annual total divided by 12) $ _____ (3)

Subtract amount provided
by allowance $(_____) (4)

Amount to come from earnings
and other sources $ _____ (5)

1. Estimate annual amount for each category.
2. Add the amounts in all categories to get an annual total.
3. Divide the annual total (2) by 12 to get monthly amount.
4. Subtract the amount the parents will provide as a monthly allowance.
5. The monthly amount (3) less the allowance amount (4) results in the amount that must be provided from earnings, gifts, and other sources.

CHART 7
Budget Worksheet: Gifts

III. Gifts	Estimated Annual Amount (1)		Total (2)
	Family	Friends	
A. Christmas	$ ___	$ ___	$ ___
B. Birthdays	$ ___	$ ___	$ ___
C. Anniversaries	$ ___	$ ___	$ ___
D. Mother's/Father's Day	$ ___	$ ___	$ ___
E. Special Occasions			
1. Graduations	$ ___	$ ___	$ ___
2. Weddings	$ ___	$ ___	$ ___
3. Valentine's Day	$ ___	$ ___	$ ___
4. Easter	$ ___	$ ___	$ ___
5. Other	$ ___	$ ___	$ ___

CHART 7 (cont.)

F. Other	$ ___	$ ___	$ ___
Annual total	$ ___	$ ___	$ ___ (2)

Monthly amount needed
(annual total divided by 12) $ ___ (3)

Subtract amount provided by allowance $(___)(4)

Amount to come from earnings
and other sources $ ___ (5)

1. Estimate annual amount for each category.
2. Add the amounts in all categories to get an annual total.
3. Divide the annual total (2) by 12 to get monthly amount.
4. Subtract the amount the parents will provide as a monthly allowance.
5. The monthly amount (3) less the allowance amount (4) results in the amount that must be provided from earnings, gifts, and other sources.

CHART 8
Monthly Plan

	Monthly Amount Needed	Allowance	Earnings, Etc.
Clothes (1)	$ ___	$ ___	$ ___
Spend	$ ___	$ ___	$ ___
Gifts	$ ___	$ ___	$ ___
Total (2)	$ ___	$ ___	$ ___
Save (10 percent of total) (2)	$ ___	$ ___	$ ___
Tithe (10 percent of total) (2)	$ ___	$ ___	$ ___
Total monthly plan (2)	$ ___	$ ___	$ ___

1. Copy totals from appropriate budget worksheets for "monthly amount needed" [worksheet line (3)], "allowance" [worksheet line (4)], and "earnings, etc." [worksheet line (5)].
2. Add to get total for each category.
3. Multiply (2) by 10 percent (or another desired percentage).
4. Multiply (2) by 10 percent (or another desired percentage).
5. Add the total (2) the save (3), and the tithe (4) amounts to determine the total monthly plan.

Parents should decide about a child working while still in high school, based on their unique circumstances and desires. Whatever the decision, it will affect the amount of the child's allowance. We (the Blues) did not require our two oldest daughters to work while they were participating in athletics or cheerleading, but once the season was over we strongly encouraged them to get a job.

Each budget category should be reviewed for each child on a regular basis; circumstances and needs change. The budget categories we've presented are good recommendations, but they're only recommendations. Give yourself time to determine the amounts needed and recognize up front that you'll need to make modifications.

If this is the first time you've used this type of system, it may take a couple of years before you're comfortable with determining the amounts per category and even with the number of categories. Remember that the *purpose* of the envelope system is not to have the perfect, inflation-adjusted, budgeted amount, but to teach your children the basic tools of money management.

How frequently you give an allowance (or funding) will depend on the ages of the children and your available income. If you begin the system with very young children, it probably should be given weekly because they can't fully comprehend how much time is in a month or a year. Most older children can be given the money on a monthly basis. For example, their clothes money for the year is divided by twelve, and given to them monthly. They then have the responsibility for the money in the envelopes, the freedom of decision making, and the freedom to fail. For some of our teens, we have given amounts on a semiannual or even annual basis, so that they can plan for and buy a wardrobe for a season.

Many parents are concerned that children will spend unwisely if they receive a large amount at one time. They may in the beginning, but that's how they're going to learn. After a series of mistakes, they'll plan much more wisely. They must have the freedom to make their own decisions and the freedom to fail.

Once the amount for each category has been determined and you're comfortable that it's a fair amount, you should not change it without a serious discussion. Be wary of manipulation by your children. If they learn they can constantly change the amount by resorting to the old argue-pout-whine method, the whole system of spending *limited* resources has been destroyed. In fact, there are no limits on the resources when you vary them according to the children's protests or desires.

The world is intent on teaching you and your children to get all you can *now*—no matter what the cost will be in the future. Credit card companies and advertising firms have this motivation. You have an awesome job trying to teach your children delayed gratification through good money management and long-range planning. Don't add to the challenges they already face each day by allowing them to have unlimited resources to meet their wants and desires. Help them learn to be responsible, mature individuals by balancing today's desires with future needs.

You don't have to require your children to keep track of where they spend the money from each envelope. The remaining amount in the envelope is the record of how much they spent. If they want to know why they're running out of money each month in a particular category and want to write down how they're spending it, that's fine. Don't be too rigid, though, in requiring them to keep track of every penny.

The amount given to children as an allowance should *definitely not* be used as a disciplinary tool. What happens if their grades go down? Do you take away their allowance? The answer is no; they still need clothes. You shouldn't use this envelope system to motivate them to get good grades. You can use other ways to accomplish those results.

Also, the allowance is not a payment for chores. As members of the family, children should perform certain chores, such as doing the dishes, cleaning their rooms, making the bed, or carrying out the trash. Children have to meet their responsibilities as members of the family, and one of those is helping with chores around the house. All members of the team must do their part.

Other chores, however, are optional. These might include raking leaves, cleaning out the garage once a year, babysitting, or doing tasks above and beyond the normal expectations of the household. For these chores your children deserve extra compensation.

In Chapter 9 we'll describe an activity that may help you decide how much your child's allowance should be. It's a special dinner with your child. We (the Blues) have used this approach ourselves. During that dinner we discussed the child's goals for the next year as well as accomplishments over the past year. To prepare for that conversation we kept a journal containing the goals. These might include meeting a new friend, making a major purchase, earning certain grades in school, achieving something specific in a sport, or spending time daily reading God's Word.

Every year we sat down with our kids to review what the allowance would be for the following year for each of the envelope categories. We also reviewed chores the child would be responsible for, both those that are expected and those that are optional for which they could earn compensation.

What the System Teaches

The system we've used is not the only system available. Feel free to take what we've shared and adapt it to your unique situation. We've found that the envelope system is a useful tool for teaching our children the following truths:

1. *Tithing.* In 1 Corinthians 16:2 we find the principles of giving, which are applicable for the New Testament church: *"On the first day of every week, each one of you should set aside a sum of money in keeping with his income, saving it up, so that when I come no collections will have to be made."*

The book of Proverbs says, *"Honor the LORD with your wealth, with the firstfruits of all your crops; then your barns will be filled to over-flowing, and your vats will brim over with new wine"* (3:9-10).

The tithe is a recognition that God owns it all. If your children put money into a Tithe envelope on a regular basis and then give it, they're learning the habit of tithing. This habit can become a meaningful way of acknowledging that ultimately God owns their money.

2. *Rewards for work.* With a limited supply of money, children must earn additional funds for the discretionary items they want. When they make such a purchase, they're receiving a significant reward for work.

3. *Savings.* Saving involves delayed gratification. Putting money into a Save envelope on a regular basis is an important discipline to ensure financial success.

Allowing some savings to be spent periodically for significant items will begin to teach your children the value of patience. Remember the definition of financial maturity—"Giving up today's desires for future benefits."

4. *Limited supply of money.* The envelope system is built on the principle that all good things come to an end. When the cookie jar or envelope is empty, the only way to get funds is to work.

Our society promises, with all the power of advertising, that you can have it all. The reality is that you can't; if you choose to consume it today, it's gone forever. That's true whether you're a child or an adult. God is the only One who's never exhausted, and never will exhaust, His resources.

5. *Opportunity cost of consumption.* When the money is gone, you can't buy anything else. There's no more dramatic way to teach the "opportunity cost" of consumption. The cost isn't dollar for dollar; multiple dollars have been taken out of the future that could have been available had the money not been spent. The envelope system makes that principle visible.

6. *Decision making.* Dealing with limited resources and unlimited possible expenditures requires that decisions be made. One

time we (the Blues) took our boys on a short trip to Disney World, even though we had our major family vacation planned for later in the summer. They took with them all the spending money they'd been saving for the main family vacation.

On our first day in Orlando, they saw lots of desirable stuffed animals and other gifts. But both realized that if they spent their money at Disney World, they wouldn't have money to spend later in the summer.

It was difficult for Judy and me not to offer advice as the boys discussed whether to buy a stuffed Mickey Mouse. But we both felt they needed to learn this lesson. They agonized over their decision. Ultimately, they made a good one—by spending some and saving some for later.

It was *their* decision, and they were learning a principle we tried to teach them. Had we given them extra money—outside the envelope system—to spend at Disney World, an important teachable moment would have been lost.

7. *Budgeting.* Budgeting is simply planning your spending. This envelope system requires thinking ahead to determine how much can be spent today.

8. *Wise buying.* Children don't have to be wise buyers for the system to work. But they'll quickly learn that by being smart shoppers they'll have more money available to do other things.

9. *Goal Setting.* Our (the Blues') boys began realizing at ages 9 and 11 that if they didn't spend the money they earned during the summers, they'd save enough to buy a car at age 16. The system teaches the wisdom and value of setting long-term as well as short-term goals.

Going Deeper

The most critical issue regarding the envelope system is that children must have *goal ownership*. In other words, it must be *their* system rather than something you impose on them. Help them set it up and understand what they can learn from it. Then allow them to have control of the money and freedom to work within the system.

You may have to change the system to fit the needs of your children. One of our (Ron and Judy's) daughters, Karen, was having trouble with the envelopes when she was 10 or 11; she prefers to live spontaneously. The five envelopes were too confining.

Karen told Judy she was fed up with the whole system. Talking with her, Judy discovered that Karen didn't feel free to spend. What she really wanted was some money to "flit" away if she chose.

Judy, with great wisdom, suggested to Karen that she add a sixth category and call it her "Flit envelope." Money in the Flit envelope could be used any way Karen chose. She already had that freedom with her Spend envelope, but didn't feel it. Merely by setting up another envelope and labeling it the way she wanted, she experienced tremendous freedom to operate within the system.

Karen has become a very disciplined young lady who does an excellent job of managing her money. I (Ron) believe some of her success resulted from the freedom she experienced when she was allowed to modify the system.

We continued the envelope system even while our kids were in college. We recalculated the amount needed each year. Thus we avoided the proverbial "Send money" pleas from college students. They knew how much pizza money they had to spend.

As strange as it may seem, boundaries are freeing. Dr. James Dobson, child psychologist and founder of Focus on the Family, tells a story that illustrates the importance of boundaries:

> Years ago, during the early days of the progressive-education movement, an enthusiastic theorist decided to take down the chain-link fence that surrounded the nursery-school yard. He thought the children would feel more freedom of movement without that visible barrier surrounding them. When the fence was removed, however, the boys and girls

huddled near the center of the play yard. Not only did they not wander away, they didn't even venture to the edge of the grounds. Clearly, there is a security for all of us in defined boundaries. That's why a child will push a parent to the point of exasperation at times. She's testing the resolve of the mother or father and exploring the limits of her world.[1]

When we know where the limits are, we can enjoy moving around within them. The envelope system provides those limits.

You may only want to use part of the system. For example, you may wish to use your allowance approach or pay for work as you've been doing. Perhaps you're already teaching your kids to save and give from those sources of income. You can adapt the envelope system by using it only for specific categories, such as clothes, or gifts for friends and family.

To wrap it all up, here's our challenge to you regarding the envelope system:

1. Discuss the system with your children and make sure they understand the extent of their responsibility.

2. Review the budgets and set the allowance/funding amounts for each of your children.

3. Give your children the file box with the money already inserted in the envelopes for the first month.

4. Be flexible!

5. Watch your children take responsibility for this very important area of their lives.

Decision-Making Concepts for Every Age

From a Child's Perspective:
Art Linkletter asked a girl of six, "Melissa, what would make a
perfect husband for you?"
And Melissa replied, "A man who could give me a lot of money
and loves horses and lets me have twenty-four kids."
"And what do you want to be when you grow up?"
"A nun."[1]

How can you tell if two adults eating dinner at a restaurant are in love?
"Just see if the man picks up the check. That's how you can tell if
he's in love."—JOHN, AGE 9

Biblical Principles:
*Better a poor but wise youth than an old but foolish king who no
longer knows how to take warning.*—ECCLESIASTES 4:13

*By wisdom a house is built, and through understanding it is estab-
lished; through knowledge its rooms are filled with rare and beautiful
treasures.*—PROVERBS 24:3-4

Children often ask us to make decisions for them.

"Should I buy these shoes?"

"Should I go to the mall with Emily?"

"What should I do?"

"How do I know?"

The way we answer these questions conveys to our children something about values, opinions, and priorities. Helping them learn to make sound decisions now will affect how they cope in their adult lives.

Decision making involves choosing among various alternatives. Failing to teach your children how to make decisions robs them of a vital skill for the process of living—financially and otherwise. Everyone is confronted daily with decisions, some more important than others.

Decision making means acting on personal objectives and priorities. For example, our (the Blues') two boys once decided they'd saved enough money to buy the bicycles they wanted. We took them to the bicycle shop, and each made a decision based on cost, color, and style. When they'd made their decisions, they'd satisfied their objectives. They didn't buy the same bicycle, however, because they had different priorities.

One of our sons asked many, many questions about our opinions. Then he chose a bicycle that neither Judy nor I would have chosen for him. That was okay, though, because *his* objectives and priorities needed to be met—not ours. In answering his questions, we tried to point him back to evaluating his real objectives and priorities. The boys were pleased with their final decisions because their objectives and priorities had been met.

Families make many important decisions through the years—what music lessons to take, summer jobs, college choices, where to go on vacation, what house to purchase, or what clothes to buy. Every decision requires making a choice from among many possibilities. The right choice is the one that satisfies the family's objectives and priorities.

Decision Making Is a Skill

Many of our activities, especially the envelope system, help your children practice making wise decisions. In addition to the basic lessons your children will learn through these activities, we hope they'll develop a more focused process for making decisions.

I (Ron) was 35 years old when someone finally introduced me to the process of decision making. I'd earned both B.A. and M.B.A. degrees, spent hours each year in continuing education, started and managed a successful business, and made two major career changes. But no one had ever taught me decision making as a process. I first learned about it when I joined Leadership Dynamics International, an organization formed specifically to teach this skill.

Through the years, I've noticed that many people instinctively make good decisions—but few understand the process they go through to make those choices. Knowing the process gives freedom and security. It provides a framework for properly evaluating options without overlooking anything.

Many years ago in a restaurant, Judy and I went through the decision-making process. The choice we made and noted on the back of a napkin led us into the financial planning business in 1979. We've never doubted that our decision put us where God wanted us. The process made clear what career I should be involved in for the rest of my life.

Training children to make decisions is equipping them to live successfully. The skill of decision making affects all areas of life, and is especially crucial in making financial choices.

Decision Making Involves a Process

A *process* is a sequence of steps leading to a result—in this case, the decision. But before you begin the process, you must avoid three common traps: the binary trap, the intuitive trap, and the voting trap.

The *binary trap* is one we face daily. It's phrased this way:
"Should I do this or not?"
"Should I buy this car or not?"
"Should I buy this house or not?"
"Should I buy this sweater or not?"
"Should I go to this college or not?"
"Should I choose this job or not?"

The binary trap has only two alternatives—to do something or not to do it. Here is the key point: A decision can never be any better than the alternatives you evaluate. If you leave yourself with only two alternatives, your decision can never be any better than those two choices. When you consider only two, you may overlook another idea that might prove the best.

You can escape the binary trap with these three questions:

1. What am I really trying to accomplish by making this decision?

2. What is the best _____? The blank could be the best use of funds, the best use of time, the best use of talent, the best whatever. Asking this question opens up the door to many *other* possibilities.

3. Are there any other alternatives? Usually there are, and your decision will be better if you consider them.

The second pit we all fall into at one time or another is the *intuitive trap*. This means that you make a decision on the basis of how you "feel" about it. If you ask others how they came to a particular decision, most will say, "I feel good about this decision," "I felt it was the right decision," or "It seemed to be the right decision." These responses indicate they intuitively made the decision.

Every decision should advance an objective, not feelings. Feelings may be indicators of objectives, but we must not confuse how we feel about an objective with the objective itself. Avoid the intuitive trap by asking these questions:

1. What are the objectives I am trying to accomplish?

2. Does each objective have the same priority? Are they all of equal importance to me?

The third snare is the *voting trap*, making a decision based on a survey of your friends. This process assumes that your advisers have the same objectives you do. They won't—hence the use of the word "trap."

Seeking counsel is certainly advisable. Wise King Solomon cautions: *"For lack of guidance a nation falls, but many advisers make victory sure"* (Proverbs 11:14). But that counsel should tell you about the validity of *your* goals and objectives; it should not take the form of a gathering of opinions with the majority ruling. You're not a politician making decisions based on the current polls.

You get out of the voting trap by asking this question: Is this *my* decision or the collective decision of my friends and counselors?

Now you are ready to get into the actual decision-making process. Here it is, in order:

1. *Write out or verbalize the actual decision to be made.* For example, write on a page, "I must decide where to live," or "I must choose the best transportation to and from work."

2. *List the objectives.* What are your main aims? To minimize cost? To maximize convenience? To improve productivity?

3. *Prioritize the objectives.* You can't have it all. Some trade-offs exist between quality vs. price, convenience vs. cost, etc. Some will be "must" priorities. The others may be nice to have, but are less important. Give each objective a number value from one to five, with five being absolutely essential and one being a nice extra.

4. *List all possible alternatives.* After you have prioritized your objectives, list possible alternatives—choices that will meet your objectives and priorities. Then ask yourself if there are any "creative alternatives." This will help you make sure you have included all the possibilities. Your decision can be no better than your best alternative.

5. *Evaluate the alternatives in light of the objectives.* For example, if I'm deciding how to get to work, one alternative may be a new

car. But if one of the objectives is for the cost to be less than $5,000, then the new car alternative is not possible. Every decision is made to accomplish certain objectives. The alternative is only good if it meets these objectives.

    6. *Choose the alternative that best meets the objectives and priorities.* Make your choice by adding up the "points" the alternatives have after evaluating them in light of the objectives.

    This process can be expanded and made more formal than what's outlined here. But just thinking through the steps and making a decision in an orderly and objective way will make you and your kids better decision makers. You'll remember what you're actually doing—meeting objectives and priorities—instead of just "alternative jumping."

    When the boys purchased their bicycles, they didn't write out their objectives and priorities. But they followed this process mentally. Judy and I had to remind ourselves that *their* objectives and priorities, not ours, needed to be met. So, when they asked for advice, we avoided giving our opinion by asking them "why" questions:

"Why do you like this style?"

"Why red?"

"Why that type of seat?"

    When our second daughter, Denise, was making her college decision, we evaluated several schools over a period of a year. We formalized the process by writing out the decision to be made. We prioritized the objectives. We listed all the possible alternatives. Finally, we evaluated those alternatives in light of the objectives.

    She initially made the decision to attend a large university. Then she was offered a basketball scholarship to a small college. When she was offered this alternative, her real objectives and priorities came clearly into focus. She realized that one very important priority was to play college basketball. She'd never considered this as an option and, therefore, had never focused on it as a high priority. When this alternative became available, we went through the process again, as outlined on the following chart.

CHART 9
Decision-Making Process

Decision: Choose a College (1)

Objectives (2)	Priorities (3)	Alternatives (4)		
		A	B	C
Location—within 2 hours of Atlanta	2	2	2	0 (5)
Size—small to medium	1	1	1	1
Variety of academic options	3	3	0	0
Cost—less than $8,000 per year	3	3	0	3
Opportunity to play basketball	5	0	0	5
Opportunity for Christian fellowship	4	4	4	4
Total	18	13	7	13 (6)

1. Define the decision to be made.
2. List the objectives.
3. Prioritize the objectives (score from 1 to 5, with 5 being absolutely essential and 1 being an optional objective).
4. List all the alternatives.
5. Score the alternatives by evaluating whether or not the alternative meets the objective (column 2). If yes, give it the priority score (column 3). If no, give it a zero.
6. Total the score for each alternative.

When we completed this decision-making chart, College A, her original choice, and College C, the small college, came out with the same score. But it was obvious to her and to us that the objective of playing basketball was an overriding priority. Her choice was clear.

The process forced her to focus on objectives and priorities instead of alternatives. The decision allowed her to meet her prioritized objectives. Normally, people make this type of decision based on an intuitive "feel" about the alternatives under consideration, not on a formal process.

Please note that her priorities were substantially different from ours and from her sister's, who had gone through the process a year earlier. This is what decision making is all about—meeting personal objectives and priorities.

Later, our younger son faced a similar difficult decision. Having been raised on this decision-making process and having tennis scholarship offers from several schools, he had a more involved list. It included five colleges and 15 criteria ranging from the school's academic reputation to the strength of the tennis coach to how pretty the girls on campus were. We were glad he gave the school's academics a higher value than the number of pretty girls he saw— but it was his objectives, not ours, that counted!

His experience provides another reason for writing down the factors involved in the decision. After he developed the list, the choice was obvious to him. But after attending his chosen college for six months, he was ready to leave. He retrieved his list to see why he went there in the first place, and realized it still was the best choice.

After remembering why he made the decision, he went on to have a successful college career there—making all-American in tennis, graduating with honors, being accepted into law school, and meeting the wonderful woman who agreed to become his wife.

Feelings change. What we're eating, how we're sleeping, the weather we endure, the music we're hearing—any little thing can sway how we feel. My son "felt good" when he made his decision.

The process encouraged him to stick with a good decision even when his feelings might have led him to make a bad one.

How to Teach

There are two types of decisions, each requiring a different teaching process. Helping your kids to master their money includes equipping them to make both kinds of choices.

Short-term, relatively unimportant decisions will be encountered on a daily basis. *Major* decisions, such as those involving college, career, or a spouse, may be once-in-a-lifetime choices. The process involving major decisions should be much more formal.

In teaching children how to make short-term decisions, it's important to remember three things.

1. Keep pointing them toward their real objectives and priorities. Encourage them to steer clear of using the phrases "I think" or "I feel." When they use those words, ask, "Why do you think or feel that way?" That nudges them to focus on the *real* objectives and helps them stay out of the intuitive trap.

2. Keep asking, "Are there any other alternatives?" This helps kids avoid the binary and intuitive traps, and to focus on a clear vision of their objectives and priorities.

3. After the decision is made, help your child evaluate his or her choice with these questions:

"Did it really accomplish your objectives?"

"Do you still like it? Why or why not?"

"Would another alternative have been better? Why didn't it come to mind?"

These questions will help them think through other options, objectives, and priorities. They remind kids to gather facts and to ask themselves, *What am I really trying to accomplish in making this decision?*

Teach your children that major decisions require a much more formal process. When making major decisions in our (the Blue) family—college, church, home, car—we put the process down on paper for consideration, revision, and future reference. We state the decision to be made, list the objectives, prioritize those objectives, list our alternatives, and then record the decision we make.

After formalizing the process and making the decision, we add a last step: evaluating the risk.

What risks are involved in a spending decision? The risk of wasting money or time. The risk of beginning a habit. The risk of distractions or physical danger.

Let's say your child wants a means of transportation, but isn't old enough to drive a car. His choices could include a bicycle, motorized scooter, moped, or go-kart.

To evaluate risk in a spending decision like this, we ask three questions:

1. What's the worst thing that can happen if we choose this option?

2. How likely is it to occur?

3. Are we willing to live with that risk?

If the answer to the last question is no, then we aren't talking about the best alternative.

We've found that sharing our own process for major family decisions with our children is an important step in teaching it to them. You give your children an invaluable tool when you teach them a decision-making process. Whether or not they use it is up to them, but if they "catch" a process from your example and teaching, they'll be more likely to make sound decisions—instead of just wondering how they "feel."

Raising Wise Guys (and Girls)

Remember, you're more likely to make a better decision when you have a longer-term perspective. Teach your children to make choices that are likely to have the best effect on the future. Help them realize that the eternal consequences of decisions are so much more important than the short term.

Another truth to teach your kids is this: Wisdom comes from God. James 1:5 states, *"If any of you lacks wisdom, he should ask God, who gives generously to all without finding fault, and it will be given to him."* Wisdom from God is necessary for each step of the process, not just at the beginning or the end. His wisdom is required to understand the real decision, the real objectives, the real priorities, and the available alternatives. Prayerful deliberation is essential to make the process work.

Help your children master the art of good financial decision making by following these three steps.

1. Allow them to make their own decisions; stop doing it for them.

2. Begin using a formalized process of decision making yourself.

3. Teach that process to your children.

Soon you'll have a better understanding of—and more confidence in—the decisions you and your child make. This skill will last both of you a lifetime.

PART II

Activities to Do with Your Children

Ready to help your kids master their money? It's time to have some fun doing just that.

In the rest of this book you'll find more than 50 learning activities to choose from. You'll be spending time with your kids anyway, right? Why not spend some of it helping them to become financially mature?

We've organized the activities by chapter to correspond to the profile of kids who master their money:

- Generous giver
- Sharp shopper
- Savvy saver
- Prudent planner
- Intelligent investor
- Willing worker

Each activity includes teaching goals, method, and age range (plus a "sweet spot" pinpointing the very best age group for that activity). A step-by-step description shows you what to do, and background information tells you why the activity is important. Many of the entries also include a "Going Deeper" section to enhance their application.

Pick the activities that will work best for your family. There's a summary of all activities at the end of the book, to help you choose and keep track of the ones you've used.

Don't try to shoehorn a whole bunch of activities into one week. Instead, become familiar with them so that when a teachable moment arrives, you can look up the applicable activities and take advantage of the opportunity.

At the start of each activity, you'll see something like this:
Teaching Method: Parents ⇨ *Intentional* ⇨ *As you go*
And this:
Their Own Experience ⇨ *Their Own Money* ⇨ *Created*
What do these mean?

They're a way of telling you what kind of approach the activity takes. The first example lets you know that in this activity, kids will be learning from you (as opposed to on their own); the teaching will be intentional (not inadvertent); and the experience will be worked into everyday events. The second example informs you that kids will learn from their own experience, using their own money, and that the event will be created or "set up" by you.

Remember that your kids will learn about money from two primary sources: (1) watching you and (2) having their own experiences with finances. Rarely will youngsters learn from a textbook about spending and saving. If they're learning from you, you're teaching inadvertently (without meaning to) or intentionally (on purpose). The latter is better; you're passing on what you *want* to pass on about what you've learned, why you save or give as you do.

Kids learn about hot and cold not just through your explanation, but more importantly by their own sense of touch. In the same way, they can learn about money through their own experiences with it—and through "experiencing" advertising, peers, or entertainment. Personal experience is the best, which is why many of the activities in this book let kids work with their own money.

Generous Givers

From a Child's Perspective:
Dear God,
If You give me a genie lamp like Aladdin, I will give anything You
   want except my money or my chess set.—RAPHAEL, AGE 8

Money is just paper and metal and if you think of it that way,
   then is it something to get greedy over? I should know because
   it happened to me when I was a kid.—DEVIN, AGE 12

An English teacher asked her third grade students, "What is the
   future tense of 'I give'?"
A boy quickly responded, "I take."

Biblical Principles:
*In everything I did, I showed you that by this kind of hard work we
must help the weak, remembering the words the Lord Jesus himself
said: "It is more blessed to give than to receive."*—ACTS 20:35

*Each man should give what he has decided in his heart to give,
not reluctantly or under compulsion, for God loves a cheerful giver.*
—2 CORINTHIANS 9:7

"Give, and it will be given to you. A good measure, pressed down, shaken together and running over, will be poured into your lap. For with the measure you use, it will be measured to you."
—LUKE 6:38

Charity Gifts for Birthday Parties

Teaching Goals:
- To reduce the dependency on material gifts for happiness at birthday parties.
- To provide experience for your children in encouraging others to give.
- To teach kids leverage in giving.
- To allow children to directly give to a charity or ministry.

Teaching Method:
- Parents ⇨ Intentional ⇨ As you go (you'd be doing birthday parties anyway)
- Their Own Experience ⇨ Their Own Money ⇨ Created

Age Range: 8-14
Sweet Spot Age Range: 9-12

Activity Description:

You need courage to try this one. Use it only if your child is mature enough to understand and "buy into" the idea; you'll be well advised to discuss it beforehand.

For your child's next birthday party, plan a fun event. However, this party won't include the traditional gift opening. When other children are invited, inform them and their parents that no gifts are to be given directly to your child. Tell them that your child has chosen a charity to which he requests all gifts be given. Ask them to bring small cash gifts in envelopes for the charity.

This activity will take some advance persuasion and subtle encouragement. You may wish to say to your child that she has plenty of "stuff" already. Chances are that she hasn't even played with some of the toys she's received at previous birthday parties. Tell her that you're going to plan a fun party for her and her friends, but that you want her to choose a charity to which others will be giving.

Be sure to make the party itself the main event. This could include games in the backyard, attending a water park, going to a skating rink, playing basketball at a gym in the winter, or visiting a pool in the summer. Have your child's favorite food there. Provide a festive atmosphere; just don't focus on gift opening.

Decorate a box—preferably a see-through container—where monetary gifts can be "deposited." Decorate the box with information about the charity your child has chosen. For example, if she has a heart for abused animals and has picked the local animal shelter, cut out magazine pictures of pets—or use brochures from the charity. Prominently display the box on a table.

After the party, total the money that was given. Take the money with your child to the chosen charity; if it must be mailed, have your child help you deposit the money and write a check.

Other parents will find this idea refreshing! In thank-you notes, let attendees know the total amount given. Don't be surprised if you receive a thank-you note from the other parents first.

Background Information:
This may appear to be a radical idea. Be assured that most other parents will support you in this; for one thing, it saves them time and effort in shopping. You may suggest a guideline gift amount—perhaps between $5 and $10, or what they would normally spend on a gift.

If your child has been invited to many birthday parties, you probably know the inconvenience of last-minute, hurried trips to the mall to buy overpriced toys for kids who probably don't need them. You've witnessed the "materialitis" that grips a child who opens present after present.

In our (the White) family, we've only been brave enough to try this on one or two occasions. The first year we had such a birthday party, our daughter was eventually enthusiastic about the idea. She'd chosen the local Christian radio station as her charity. She was becoming more interested in Christian music; while listening to the radio she'd heard the station's appeals for money.

After the party, I went with her to the radio station. When we lifted the jar of money and explained our fund raising idea, the staff was very appreciative.

The station's personnel provided much positive and public praise to our daughter. It was helpful to hear the truths we were trying to teach being reiterated by other respected adults.

Our daughter was thrilled to get an in-depth tour of the station. She even saw the production room and put on headphones as though she were on the radio.

Going Deeper:

Another benefit of this activity is that your children begin to see leverage at work when many people donate to a good cause. Through your child's efforts (and sacrifice), the attendees give more in total than your child could do on her own.

Encourage your child to think of other examples where her influence might be leveraged to encourage many others to give to an important cause.

Head Up a Giving Foundation

Teaching Goals:
- To allow kids to decide a portion of the family's giving budget.
- To experience the joy of giving more substantial amounts.
- To practice the decision-making process of deciding how and where to give.

Teaching Method:
 • Parents ⇨ Intentional ⇨ Created
Age Range: 6-18
Sweet Spot Age Range: 8-16

Activity Description:
During your family meeting or devotion time, announce to your children that you need their help in deciding where your family gives. Explain to them how you currently give to your church and how contributing to God's kingdom work through the local church is your first giving priority. You may further explain that there are opportunities to give beyond the church.

Explain that you and your spouse have decided to give additional amounts—and you're going to assign to your kids the responsibility of deciding where that money goes. Tell them the amount over which you've decided to give them control. It might be $100 or $250 for the year. Or, you may decide to allow them to control $15 or $20 per month.

Ask your kids to think about areas in which they're interested, where the needs are, and to what organizations they might give in order to provide for those needs. Allow them time—a week, perhaps—to think and pray about this. Tell them that they'll present their ideas at your next family meeting.

When that time comes, have each child present his or her ideas and the reasons for choosing causes or organizations. It's important that you and other family members don't criticize or immediately dismiss an organization or cause. Part of the value of the activity is for you to see where your child's heart lies and what areas he seems to have a passion for.

Your children may have picked a cause but not yet identified an organization. This can develop into an important teaching activity if you show them how to research organizations. A child who's concerned about orphans in foreign countries could do research on those who help families adopt orphans or who minister to orphans.

If your child has a friend who's deaf and is concerned about others who can't hear, you may find groups that school or otherwise care for the hearing impaired.

Ask your child (or help her) to research the organizations. This can be done through an Internet search. When you find likely and reputable groups, you can call or e-mail to find out how they might use financial help. You should also ask if the organization is a member of a group such as the ECFA (Evangelical Council for Financial Accountability).

When you sign up, send money, or pledge support to the organizations your child chooses, try to have his name listed as the contact. You may be the one writing the check, but his name will assure him the thrill of getting mail addressed to him for a thank-you or acknowledgment.

Background Information:

In my (Jeremy's) family, we began a tradition at Christmastime involving the kids in how to give a very special gift to Jesus. We'd felt strongly that we shouldn't go overboard in our Christmas giving to each other, so we decided to give more to Jesus than the largest single gift we give to a family member or to anyone else.

We began to involve our kids in deciding where to give additional monies. Some years we give to a needy family, some years to the local crisis pregnancy center, and some years to Project Angel Tree (a ministry providing Christmas gifts to children whose parents are in prison).

Our kids thoroughly enjoy this activity at Christmastime. We decided to expand it beyond that season, not wanting to leave the impression that Christmas is the only time we consider giving to others.

When I announced this activity and challenged our kids to decide where they had a heart and a passion to give some of our family money, they were very excited. We told them they could decide where to send $350 for the year. We explained that this was in addition to our tithe to our church, and in addition to the other ministries we were supporting.

When we met for our follow-up family meeting, we were pleased with the decisions and the process that our kids followed. One daughter decided to give to a world relief organization that produces a catalog from which you can "shop" for items such as a goat to feed a family of four. Because my daughter's grandparents raise goats, she was interested in giving these animals to a family so they could have milk and a herd to support themselves. She also gave money for hygiene kits for children, Bibles in native languages, and equipment such as soccer balls. I was quite amazed at how far our $350 went with these organizations.

Our other daughter wanted to sponsor a child. As a family we'd been supporting a child through Compassion International for several years; this daughter wanted to sponsor her own. She went on the Compassion Web site and was able to select the country, gender, and age of the child. She wanted to be able to write to and begin a relationship with both children.

Going Deeper:
Giving includes more than money. Why not set a goal to support one local ministry, such as a pregnancy resource center, with finances, time, fund raising, getting others involved, or donating other skills? You can involve the whole family in meaningful community service rather than just sending a check.

<hr/>

Candy, Dolls, Army Men, and Proportions

Teaching Goals:
• To illustrate the prosperity and relative material advantage your children enjoy.

- To increase appreciation for their blessings.
- To motivate sharing and giving out of your children's abundance.

Teaching Method:
- Parents ⇨ Intentional ⇨ Created

Age Range: 4-12
Sweet Spot Age Range: 5-8

Activity Description:

Rather than boring and overwhelming children with statistics, use visual aids to represent groups of people with vastly different and disproportional amounts of food, water, and money.

Using small plastic animals, green army men, or similar objects, represent three groups of people as described in the following chart. Next to each group, put the following items in the proportions listed.

As you're separating and allocating the items to each people group, explain, "This small group gets this food. This big group gets this small amount of money."

After dividing up the items, let your kids observe the obvious disproportion. Explain that the number of plastic animals or army men represents the number of people in different parts of the world. For example, the United States has only about 5 out of every 100 people (5 percent) in the world, yet has more money, food, and "drinks" than most countries.

Explain that your children didn't choose where to be born. God made the choice. If they live in a prosperous country, they should feel fortunate. God doesn't love them more than He loves children in other places; He just allowed them to be born where they were born.

Ask your kids, "If God loves all of His children equally, but has given more to one group of children, what would He expect that group to do?"

By asking this open-ended question, you can gain insight into your kids and provide teaching opportunities. They may respond

People and Resources	United States	Other Developed Countries (in Europe, for example)	Developing Countries (many African countries, for example)
Population (represented by dolls, army men, or other figures)	About 5 percent	About 20 percent	About 75 percent
Food (represented by candy such as Skittles or M&Ms)	1/2 package	1/4 package	1/4 package
Water (represented by soda, water, or other drinks)	Gallon of water + several cans of soda	Couple of bottles of water + one can of soda	Glass of slightly muddy water
Money	30 pennies + 2 dollar bills + a few quarters + 3 nickels	Quarter + dime + nickel	Pennies

with, "He would expect them to be thankful or to pray for the others." Probably the most common answer would be that He would expect them to share. Talk about the Bible verse *"From everyone who has been given much, much will be demanded"* (Luke 12:48).

Background Information:
UNICEF estimates that in the United States, more people die from obesity-related causes than in the other six most developed countries. About 40 percent of the world's obesity-related deaths occur in the United States. The average U.S. adult consumes 50 percent more calories than the average person worldwide.

In contrast, of the estimated 6.5 billion people in the world, 1.2 billion lack access to safe drinking water. Every day, over 850 million people worldwide go hungry.

The aim of this activity is not to burden sensitive children with guilt, but to point out the blessings many kids enjoy and often take for granted. Recognizing blessings can lead to a spirit of thankfulness and a desire to share them.

Going Deeper:
In addition to using army men and candy, you can use other means to illustrate the fact that most children in developed countries are better off than many other children in the world. For example, you could use building blocks to build bigger houses for those in developed countries and smaller houses for those in less developed nations.

The Blessing List: an Anti-Envy Tool

Teaching Goals:
  • To count the many blessings your children enjoy.
  • To help them not to take their blessings for granted.
  • To defend against envy and coveting.
Teaching Method:
  • Parents ⇨ Intentional ⇨ Created
Age Range: 6-18
Sweet Spot Age Range: 10-18

Activity Description:
Try a simple but powerful activity with your kids. Have them write their own "Blessing List." Lead by example and complete your list first. The instructions are simple: Write a list of blessings that God has given you. You can copy and use the form that follows. For a longer list, use more than one copy.

My Blessing List
"Count your many blessings,
name them one by one
and it will surprise you
what the Lord has done."
—JOHNSON OATMAN, JR.

1. _____

2. _____

3. _____

4. _____

5. _____

6. _____

7. _____

8. _____

9. _____

10. _____

11. _____

12. _____

13. _____

14. _____

15. _____

"Praise the LORD, O my soul,
and forget not all his benefits."
—PSALM 103:2

List specific blessings unique to your family—not the general ones commonly recited in prayer (good health, freedom, etc.). For you, the parent, a blessing may be your child's unique laugh, your spouse's meaningful hugs, the health to play your favorite sport, experiencing God's creation in the fall, and so on.

Have your children complete their lists. Talk with them about mentioning specific blessings: enjoying Grandma's homemade chocolate chip cookies and milk, knowing how to ride a bicycle without training wheels, having their own bedroom, etc. They may mention people by name or certain toys. That's fine. You may need to "take dictation" from younger children, say ages 6-9, but older children should write down their blessings themselves.

The process of completing the Blessing List is valuable itself. Let's take the application a bit further, though.

Review the list with your child and affirm him. Agree with him about how blessed he is. Ask these questions for discussion:

• What did you realize after completing and looking over your Blessing List?
• If you had enough time and paper, you could probably think of more—like clean water, air to breathe, a cool house in the summer and a warm one in winter, electricity, and so on. Would you give up all the items on your list for money?
• Where do your blessings come from?
• How do you think God feels when we complain about not having something?
• How can this list help your attitude?

Make a couple of copies of the list. Have your child keep a copy of the list in his or her purse, backpack, or other accessible place. When your child is going through the blues, had a disappointing day, or is constantly whining about not having enough things, pull out the Blessing List. Have him read over it. When your child is envious of friends, remind him of all the blessings he has.

Background Information:
Many financial planners neglect the importance of attitudes in money-related decisions. They may recommend wise actions, but our strong desires for approval and instant gratification lead us astray to buy cars, houses, or clothes we can't afford. Tackling your financial challenges as an adult requires tackling attitudes such as envy.

We have to admit that it's hard to escape the long reach of envy—even at church. Think about this battle on a typical Sunday. We park next to someone with a nicer car. We admire the way others are dressed in Sunday school. While walking to the worship service, we overhear someone talking about an exotic vacation. We sit behind someone in the service and wish we had her jewelry.

Envy motivates us to want more and more. It robs us of peace and thankfulness. It distracts us from worshiping God and causes us, in effect, to worship things.

Kids face the envy and coveting battles just as we parents do. We merely hide it better. We work it subtly into our rationales for buying something. Kids just pout, whine, or complain.

God is surely disappointed when we don't appreciate what we have. Chances are that, despite your financial challenges, five or six billion people would do just about anything to trade economic positions with you.

This activity can help you and your child guard against envy, honor God, draw closer to Him, become more thankful and content, and avoid making unwise financial decisions. We're confident that you wouldn't want to trade your Blessing List for anyone else's. Teach the same to your kids.

Plan a Family Mission Project

Teaching Goals:
- To learn about giving time and service in addition to money.
- To help your children appreciate the blessings they have.

- To provide your kids the experience of seeing and meeting people in less fortunate circumstances.

Teaching Method:
- Parents ⇨ Intentional ⇨ Created
- Their Own Experience ⇨ Others

Age Range: 8-18
Sweet Spot Age Range: 10-16

Activity Description:
Organize a family mission project. We don't necessarily mean traipsing off to the jungle. Simply give your kids contact with people who have more physical and economic needs than your family does.

Have your kids ever been in the house of a much needier person? How much time have they spent with disabled people? Have they visited an elderly person who has difficulty keeping up his or her property or is living alone?

Here are a few examples of local projects (the names and opportunities may vary in your community) to engage your family's energy:

- Deliver meals for a food ministry or "Meals on Wheels" project.
- Volunteer to serve food in a soup kitchen, rescue mission, or homeless shelter.
- Join a Habitat for Humanity or similar organization's building project.
- Contact your church staff or benevolence committee to find out about needy families or shut-ins. Deliver homemade cookies and cards to them. Take a basket of groceries and household items.

Moving beyond your local community, here are some other ideas:

- Sponsor a needy child in another country through an organization like Compassion International or World Vision.

• Take a family trip under the guidance of a missionary organization. To encourage philanthropy, go to Africa and see what a freshly dug well will do for a community.

Background Information:
The best cure for "affluenza"—that very contagious materialistic fever—is giving. Giving not only money, but also time and effort, tends to inoculate us against our selfish tendencies.

When my (Jeremy's) kids were younger, our accounting and investment firm became more successful and our income increased. Gratefully, I was able to provide a nice place to live, pleasant neighborhoods, and wonderful vacations. Our children's friends lived in nice houses, too. Our church had built a beautiful children's building. Everywhere our kids played, shopped, worshiped, or ate was very comfortable.

Although I had often prayed, "Lord, may my children not take their blessings for granted," I felt we should be engineering some doses of reality. Our family began delivering meals for a local food ministry regularly. Once a week, every week, all four of us take a hot meal and day-old bread, donated by local grocery stores, to elderly people, single mothers in housing projects, disabled men, and lonely widows.

This is not a "kids only" project for school; it's a family service project. We all work in it. I've tried to help consistently, even during some of my busiest work times.

I'm not claiming that we're a perfect little family, of course. My kids are kids. They don't disguise their true feelings as well as adults do. They grimace when the lady with a foul odor asks for a hug. They gripe about how long an older person takes to tell a story we've heard six times before. They try to avoid going into the house where the roaches are so comfortable and in charge that they come out and greet us upon arrival.

I can't say this activity has caused our kids to forsake every mall and ask to do social work instead. But we have a reference point—

not to put others down, but to appreciate our material blessings. When my kids read what Jesus said about the poor and needy, they have a better understanding of what that means. When they read what Paul wrote about sharing from our abundance with others during times of need, they can see that they have an abundance compared with others.

This experience gives us more opportunities for other "as you go" teaching moments. We talk about the foolishness of having a big-screen TV with satellite programming while living in a collapsing house with two cars in the front yard that don't run. We observe that a woman overcame cystic fibrosis and the label of "retarded" to live on her own in the cleanest, neatest apartment of any housing project we've seen.

It's easy to exaggerate the difficulty of doing such a project: "Oh, we can't commit regularly." "It's not the right time." Yet many of us will spend far more time planning our next camping trip or vacation.

Camping and vacations are wonderful. But the family bonding that happens during those times can happen with a family mission project as well.

Matching Gift Program

Teaching Goals:
- To see how money can be leveraged to support important causes.
- To encourage your children to engage in intentional giving.
- To track and keep up with the gifts given during a period of time.

Teaching Method:
- Their Own Experience ⇨ Their Own Money ⇨ Created

Age Range: 8-18
Sweet Spot Age Range: 12-15

Activity Description:
Announce to your children that you're establishing a matching gift program (or "challenge" grant). On first hearing this idea, your kids may think they're going to be receiving gifts that match or a matching set of clothes. Explain, using the simplest terms you can, that many private companies and other donors offer to help raise funds for organizations. To encourage giving to a certain organization, a corporation or individuals will match every dollar given to that group.

Reveal that during the next month, season, or year, you'll match dollar for dollar the gift your child gives of her own money to your church, a selected ministry, or other causes. For example, if she's giving from her allowance or earnings from work, you'll add the same amount. To qualify for this match, she'll have to provide you a detailed record of her giving during this period of time.

At the end of the time period, ask your child to present to you her reasons for her donations. Then you can send a check to the organization. When you do that, include a brief letter explaining that you're matching the gifts of your child.

In the letter, praise your child to the organization, explaining how she worked hard and gave of her own money/allowance because she feels this organization is important. Explain that you're giving an additional gift in honor of your child's efforts. The organization probably will be surprised and may go to great lengths to express appreciation.

Background Information:
Many organizations have used challenge gifts, challenge grants, and matching gifts as a way to leverage and increase their base of donors. As your children become adults, they'll likely have opportunities to participate in a building campaign or employer's matching gift program. This activity introduces the concept of "leverage"—using your small weight wisely to lift a larger one—and could even motivate your child to become the sponsor of a challenge.

Think of it: Your child might grow into an adult who empowers and challenges others to give. You might be training God's next great philanthropist!

Going Deeper:
Older teenage children, especially those with an income from a job, may wish to challenge their siblings by matching funds. Let's say your 16-year-old has been regularly earning money from mowing yards or babysitting. Your family has learned of a specific need from a missionary you know personally. As a family, you may decide to offer a challenge grant or encourage others to do so. The 16-year-old could tell her siblings, "For every dollar you set aside in the next month for this missionary, I will give [50 cents, $2, etc.]."

This activity and its variations encourage family unity and cooperation; the kids are working toward the same goal, and that goal is giving.

We're sure you've seen jealousy raise its ugly head when one sibling is saving for a special personal item and has more money than the others. Even having a bigger goal can sometimes cause a fight! When it comes to giving, involve all the kids and encourage them to encourage one another. We hope that for you, as it has for us, this mutual love of giving will produce great results in each child and bonding as a family.

Read Books, Watch Videos about Giving

Teaching Goal:
- To inspire your kids toward generous giving and philanthropy.

Teaching Method:
- Their Own Experience ⇨ Others

Age Range: Various

Activity Description:
From inspiring autobiographies of generous givers to entertaining kids' stories, these resources can back you up on your teaching. The books marked with an asterisk (*) would make excellent choices for more advanced reading.

Title: *Mover of Men and Mountains: The Autobiography of R.G. LeTourneau**
Author: R. G. LeTourneau (Moody Publishers, 1967)
Description: Your Tonka-loving boys who enjoy playing in the dirt, and your aspiring entrepreneurs, will enjoy this autobiography. Mr. LeTourneau, holder of 297 patents, invented the bulldozer, scrapers, and dump wagons. His company built 70 percent of the heavy earthmoving equipment used by Allied forces in World War II. He also used his extraordinary business skills and creativity to further the missionary work of the Great Commission. LeTourneau gave 90 percent of his personal and business income to the Lord's work.
Length: 290 pages
Age Range: 10-18

Title: *The Treasure Principle**
Author: Randy Alcorn (Multnomah Publishers, 2001)
Description: "The Treasure Principle," taught in the Bible but widely neglected today, is just this: When it comes to money, you can't take it with you—but you can send it on ahead. In this pocket-sized book, pastor and author Randy Alcorn urges Christians to store up treasures for themselves in their true home: heaven. The single greatest obstacle to generous giving, he argues, is the illusion that this world is really our home. We cling so tightly to our wealth on earth because we worry about building security here.
Length: 96 pages
Age Range: 12-18

Title: *Giving Warriors: Inspirational Stories of Men and Women Who Experienced the Joy of Giving* (DVD)
Author: Produced by Generous Giving, 2003
Description: This DVD contains eight three-minute vignettes that capture the amazing stories of great givers from history—men and women whose wealth God used to stir spiritual awakenings in their respective times. Included are the stories of Quaker Oats founder Henry Parsons Crowell, R. G. LeTourneau, John Wesley, Stanley Tam, Walter and Ralph Meloon, Francis of Assisi, and Katharine Drexel, plus an interview with Campus Crusade for Christ founders Bill and Vonette Bright on how their "Contract with God" radically changed their lives.
Length: 45 minutes
Age Range: 12-18

Title: *What If I Owned Everything?*
Author: Larry Burkett (Thomas Nelson, 1997)
Description: This simple, entertaining story teaches Scripture-based financial principles in a way that helps kids learn the basics of stewardship. It starts when Jenny and Jeremy challenge each other to the "longest, most unbelievable Better-Than-Best Match-Off in all of history." Their imaginations run wild—revealing the dangers of greed, the fun of sharing, and the joy of being content with what God has entrusted to us.
Length: 32 pages
Age Range: 4-10

Title: *A Chair for My Mother*
Author: Vera B. Williams (Greenwillow Books, 1982)
Description: A family loses all its furniture in a fire. The goal is to buy a chair for Mother. Find out how the family, neighbors, and friends work together for success.
Length: 28 pages
Age Range: 6-11

Title: VeggieTales: *The Toy That Saved Christmas* (video)
Author: Big Idea Productions, 1998
Description: Appropriate for Christmas or at other times. Greedy Wally P. Nezzer has convinced all of Dinkletown that "Christmas is when you get stuff!" As children whine for more toys, one brave little Buzz-Saw Louie doll decides to step in. Bob the Tomato, Larry the Cucumber, and Junior Asparagus help Louie spread the word that "Christmas isn't about getting—it's about giving. And it's especially about a little Baby who was the greatest Gift of all!"
Length: 30 minutes
Age Range: 3-11

Title: *The Giving Tree*
Author: Shel Silverstein (Harper & Row, 1964)
Description: This is a sensitive tale of giving (and taking) until there is no more to give—or so it seems. A subtle yet touching reminder of how Jesus sacrificed everything and gave to us.
Length: 48 pages
Age Range: All ages

Title: *Notable American Philanthropists**
Author: Edited by Robert T. Grimm, Jr. (Greenwood Press, 2002)
Description: This book provides substantial profiles of individuals and families (Kelloggs, Carnegies, Mellons, etc.) who made outstanding philanthropic contributions from the 1600s to the present. The 78 entries describe 110 individuals. Excellent reference book for reports and research on well-known figures. Particular attention is paid to an individual's motivations.
Length: 416 pages
Age Range: 14-18

Title: *King Midas*
Author: Nathaniel Hawthorne (McGraw-Hill, 1959)

Description: Based on the Greek legend. King Midas was a greedy ruler who wished everything he touched would turn to gold. He got his wish, but found out that some things are more precious than gold.

Length: 29 pages

Age Range: 5-12

Going Deeper:

For younger children, consider reading aloud the age-appropriate books and discussing them.

For older children, consider assigning the books to read. Give them a financial reward if they read the book and write a report for you. One of my (Jeremy's) clients offered his 17-year-old daughter $500 to be invested in a mutual fund if she read Dave Ramsey's book *Financial Peace* (recommended in chapter 9) and wrote a summary of what she learned.

Sharp Shoppers

From a Child's Perspective:

"Why don't you get some expensive money?" —Three-year-old daughter, when told by her mother that she could not get the toys asked for because they were too expensive.[1]

If you go to the mall and you want to buy something right away, you should go and find something else before you decide to buy the first thing you see!—JENNY, AGE 7

I say that everything you want and can afford, I think you should buy it.—JASON, AGE 10

Biblical Principles:

She selects wool and flax and works with eager hands. She is like the merchant ships, bringing her food from afar. . . . She sees that her trading is profitable. . . .

    When it snows, she has no fear for her household; for all of them are clothed in scarlet. . . . She watches over the affairs of her household. . . . Her children arise and call her blessed; her husband also, and he praises her.—PROVERBS 31:13-14, 18, 21, 27, 28

Currency Exchange

Teaching Goals:
 • To help kids appreciate the value of a dollar.
 • To understand relative value by converting the cost of items into work units or allowance units.

Teaching Method:
 • Parents ➪ Intentional ➪ As You Go
 • Their Own Experience ➪ Their Own Money ➪ As You Go

Age Range: 8-18

Sweet Spot Age Range: 10-18

Activity Description:

Most parents have struggled with teaching their children the value of money. It's so frustrating when your child hears the cost of something—say, $20—and replies, "Oh, that's not very much."

To help your children translate the cost of items into terms they can understand, convert the cost into work units. What we mean by "work units" is the amount of time they must work to earn that much money.

If your daughter earns $5 per hour babysitting, translate the price of the costume jewelry she wants to buy into babysitting hours. Then pose the question, "Honey, are the bracelets, lip gloss, and purse worth four hours of babysitting?"

Even better, personalize it. "Are these items worth putting up with the Benson kids for four hours while you miss your favorite TV show?" With this approach, you're no longer the grinch who always says no. You're empowering your child to choose what she wants.

"Son, is that DVD worth the two hours it took you to mow Mrs. Smith's yard? Remember how you sweated and had to pull the weeds from her landscaping, too?"

This approach can also be used with allowances. "Jacob, you have some spending money. Just think of it this way: Buying that toy will cost five weeks of allowance. Is that what you want?"

Warning: This conversion activity sounds logical to us adults. But most kids, pondering your question and holding the shiny, new, desired object, will almost always choose the toy in hand. Think of not-so-rational decisions you've made while intoxicated with that new-car smell and the feel of "rich, Corinthian leather"!

Your kids may make some foolish decisions at first (and you'll still retain veto power over their purchases), but keep at it. Over time, they'll think longer and harder about their choices.

Background Information:
Our (the White) family was planning a Florida vacation after my busy tax season. My parents wanted to give my kids an opportunity to earn spending money for the trip.

The grandparents paid $1 for every gate that my children painted on the farm. My kids worked diligently brushing aluminum paint onto 16 gates, each 10 feet long. Under straw hats they sweated, swatted bugs, and got paint on their hands.

Watch out, Florida; these kids had $16 in their pockets to burn.

During our stops at numerous tourist traps and souvenir shops, my children repeated the same refrain: "Can I buy this? It's only $5."

My "currency exchange translator" gave me a great response: "Think about this. Is this item worth the amount of work it took to paint five gates on the farm?"

I could see the wheels turning in their heads as they considered the value of the purchase. It worked. They said "no" more often to themselves, and I didn't have to be the bad guy.

This idea may not work as well with allowances. But consider extra chores or projects to become the "currency exchange."

Going Deeper:
Consider that next purchase at Wal-Mart for $100. Is that worth "x" number of hours of your work?

Think of this on a "net" basis. After taxes, after the cost of commuting, after work clothes and other work expenses, what do you earn per hour? Use that result to compute whether the extra options on the car are worth it or if you need a fourth TV in the house.

Buying Consultant

Teaching Goals:
   • To allow your children to express the wisdom they've gained about making purchases.
   • To hold them accountable for following their own advice.

Teaching Method:
   • Parents ➪ Intentional ➪ As You Go
   • Their Own Experience ➪ Their Own Money ➪ As You Go

Age Range: 8-16
Sweet Spot Age Range: 10-14

Activity Description:

Tell your children you need to consult with them; you need to tap into their wisdom. Present the following scenario to them.

A young person has just arrived in your developed country from a distant, poorer country. He has no experience in shopping at our stores, no history in handling money, and no idea how to shop wisely. He would like a list of useful tips when he goes shopping. What "buying smarts" would your children give him?

Don't tell your kids how to answer. Note everything they say; have them date the sheet and sign it. Congratulate them on the excellent tips. Encourage them by admitting that you didn't realize how much they already knew.

Make copies of the list and keep it available. Save it so that you can use it down the road—perhaps when a child goes off to college or is about to spend a substantial sum. You can whip it out on the spot when your children are about to make a poor spending decision. You can make a copy and give it to them to keep with their money or budget information.

Background Information:
During lunch one Sunday, we (Ron and Judy) asked our children for their ideas on how to buy wisely. We offered no insight or encouragement; we merely recorded what they had to say. Here is what they've learned through experience and guidance:

- Watch for sales.
- Buy quality.
- Before you go shopping, set a dollar limit on what you'll spend, and take only that amount with you.
- Don't browse—contrary to the popular motto, "Shop 'til you drop."
- Never take credit cards on a shopping trip.
- Wait two days on an impulse purchase.
- Plan what you'll buy.
- Live by your budget.
- Think about the purchase.
- When buying clothes, make a list of what you have before going shopping; in other words, take an inventory. Decide what will go with the rest of your wardrobe and shop for specifics. Don't just shop for whatever catches your eye.
- Always get advice from brothers or sisters or parents before buying.

These were their ideas. Quite frankly, when I read through the list, I realized how often I don't follow these rules. Children really can be both wise and teachable.

After hearing Ron describe this activity, I (Jeremy) tried it with my own children. I, too, was pleasantly surprised by their responses. Here's what they said:

- Save your money, then go shopping.
- Research your item for best price and quality.
- Buy the one you like the best.
- Don't just buy the one that is cheapest, but look for quality.
- If you find the one that's cheapest, but not very good quality, wait. Don't buy it then, but wait until later.

- Don't buy something that costs a lot of money just because your friends have it. Buy something you'll use.
- Compare prices on the Internet.

Sometimes we don't give our kids credit for how much they know or give ourselves credit for how much we've already taught them. It seems like they already know how to be wise shoppers. So now my goal is to remind them of what they already know. Wisdom is simply knowledge applied to life.

Going Deeper:

Type up your children's list of ideas for making wise purchases. Reduce the size of the list so that it can fit easily in their purses or wallets. Next time they want to make an impulse purchase, they'll have their list handy.

How Much Does It Really Cost?

Teaching Goals:
- To teach the total cost of a purchase including interest.
- To improve discernment in making financial decisions.

Teaching Method:
- Parents ⇨ Intentional ⇨ Created

Age Range: 10-18
Sweet Spot Age Range: 12-15

Activity Description:

This activity will compute the interest cost of financing.

Pull out the Sunday paper classified section with the vehicle dealership ads. Choose advertisements in which monthly payments are emphasized. You may also choose inserts for stores offering large-screen televisions or other high-priced electronic items on credit.

Using the ad, ask your child these questions:

1. If you bought one of these items, what would your monthly payment be?

2. How long do you make those monthly payments? (Sometimes this is difficult to find. You may have to search the fine print with your child.)

3. Why do you think the advertisement shows the monthly payment in a big font, but has the purchase price (or the number of months) in a little font?

4. Compute the total amount of your payments if you paid the monthly payments. (Explain that this is the number of months the payments are to be made multiplied by the monthly payment.)

5. What is the purchase price if you save up your money and buy the item without making monthly payments? (You may have to do some independent research to find the regular purchase price.)

6. What is the difference between the total purchase price if you saved and bought it and the total of the monthly payments?

Background Information:
Advertisers of cars, big-screen TVs, and boats rarely mention the actual purchase price. They say, "Only $399 per month." They also rarely mention how many months the buyer must pay that "low, low monthly payment."

Unfortunately, this tactic has succeeded. Many people fall into thinking, "Oh, I can afford that monthly payment." The result in the U.S. is that consumer debt, meaning nonmortgage debt, recently has been near all-time highs despite a relatively strong economy.

Your kids can do better. By following through on this activity, you create an awareness of this advertising trap. Help kids form the habit of thinking of purchases in terms of the total price. When they're thinking of buying an expensive item, have them evaluate the purchase based on this price, and encourage them to save toward it.

Going Deeper:

Consider assigning your child the task of finding five other advertisements using monthly payments. Offer an incentive (a trip to your favorite ice cream store or a $5 bonus) if they locate other examples and compute the differences correctly.

Emphasize again the value of saving for what you want. When you save, you get to keep the difference between the total amount paid with monthly payments and the purchase price.

Discuss how the car companies' or electronic stores' desire to "earn" interest is a direct cost to the buyer.

Advertising Detectives

Teaching Goals:
- To teach discernment about the aims of advertising.
- To begin the habit of thinking through the arguments of the advertising pitch.

Teaching Method:
- Parents ⇨ Intentional ⇨ As You Go

Age Range: 7-14
Sweet Spot Age Range: 9-12

Activity Description:

Next time you're watching the news, cartoons, or sports, discuss the commercials with your child. For fathers, particularly, it may be difficult to keep your fingers off the remote control. Try to sit through a commercial and talk about it with your child.

Pretend that the two of you are detectives searching for clues. You're watching closely to see how the commercial tries to convince or persuade you. Here are some discussion questions:

- What method does the commercial use to get your attention? (Humor, a celebrity, beautiful scenery, a short story, and so on)

- How does the advertiser try to make its product seem cool?
- How does the advertiser try to make you feel bad because you don't have the product?
- How does the advertiser say your life will improve with this product?
- What may have been exaggerated in the commercial? What are the partial truths?
- What may be alternatives to this product?

Begin this activity with television commercials because they tend to offer plenty of images, sound, and action. Later, you can expand to radio commercials, billboards, and magazine advertisements.

Background Information:
When speaking at financial seminars, I (Jeremy) often ask the audience, "Do you think it's more difficult to manage your money wisely now than it was 50 years ago?" Most people respond that it's more difficult now.

I then follow up with the question, "Why do you think that's so?" Responses typically include the availability of credit cards, more stuff to buy, easier credit terms on loans, more affluence, and the onslaught of advertising.

Consider that today's parents belong to the first generation to be bombarded with advertisements constantly from birth! TV, radio, billboards, clothing, junk mail, bus signs—ads have been around you for your entire life. Your children face these now-traditional pitches plus even more insidious, invasive, nearly omnipresent ads through e-mail, the Internet, product placements in movies, and infomercials.

Your children need to be armed to discern and defend against this onslaught. You can educate them about how advertising is necessary to pay for or sponsor "free" things, such as radio or network television or Internet search engines. It's a way in which companies try to spread the word about a new product or service. Make sure younger children understand the difference between the commercial on TV and the content of the program.

Advertisers try to get attention. They try to stand out from competition. They may stretch the truth, present only the positive studies, use statistics in a confusing way, use celebrities who are paid to say good things, or present unrealistic scenarios.

You must tell your children they simply can't believe everything they see or hear in advertisements. Point out that chewing a certain gum will not instantly give your child scores of friends or white teeth like those of the touched-up model in the ad.

Discuss with children how advertisers appeal to our emotions and our desire to be liked. So much of the implied messages of advertising can be summarized by the following:

- You'll be cool, like celebrity "X," when you buy the product.
- You deserve it.
- If you use this product, you'll have fame, power, beauty, or wealth.
- Being able to afford it means being able to afford the payments, not necessarily the *real* cost.
- You can buy it now and enjoy it while you pay for it.
- Deny yourself nothing. If it looks, feels, smells, or sounds good to you, go for it.
- You owe it to yourself.
- Be like everyone else, especially the popular people.
- Live for today. Don't wait for tomorrow.

Going Deeper:

With younger children, use the advertisements for products they're familiar with, such as those promoted in Saturday morning cartoon commercials.

With younger children or even older, don't use ads for products they don't understand, such as medicine for incontinence or Medicare supplemental insurance. You'll get bogged down in trying to explain the product and lose the meaning of the activity. (Don't you hate watching a football game with your child and trying to explain the disclaimers for sexual enhancement medications?)

Though we try to turn off commercials most of the time—particularly those advertising beer—they can be used as teaching moments. On occasion, let your 12-year-old see a beer commercial. Observe that the commercial doesn't show the victims of drunk driving fatalities. It doesn't show the women and children abused by alcoholics. No mention is made of the many young people losing their schooling, careers, or families to alcohol abuse. Let's make sure we all keep our thinking caps on while the commercials run.

Food Court Funding

Teaching Goals:
  • To teach kids how to allocate spending within boundaries.
  • To give them experience with minor decision making.
Teaching Method:
  • Parents ⇨ Intentional ⇨ As You Go
Age Range: 8-16
Sweet Spot Age Range: 9-14

Activity Description:
Give your kids a predetermined amount to spend at a mall food court. Set the amount high enough to have a decent meal, but not so high to be able to order the super-sizes of every option including two desserts. Go over any family rules you have (such as no soft drinks). Remind kids that this is their meal—no supplements later. Then tell them they can decide what to get.

This also can be an opportunity to learn about taxes. Remind kids about sales tax being added to the purchase (where applicable).

Let children order and pay the cashier. Perhaps you'll want to stand at a distance to observe the transaction. Most kids feel "big and grown-up" doing this by themselves.

Besides teaching principles of smart shopping, you'll be amazed at how this activity reduces dining-out conflict. You won't be the bad guy, saying, "No, that's too much," or, "We're not going to spend that on a burger."

Background Information:

Do your kids ever wear you out at fast-food restaurants? Are those food courts in the malls a convenience or a cacophony of over-whelming choices?

In many families, one child always seems to want the most expensive food item on the menu; another is more interested in a big drink. One loves chicken nuggets while another just wants fries and a prize.

I (Jeremy), being of sound mind and tight wallet, began to real-ize how I was perceived as a Grinch at restaurants. The kids would tell me what they wanted. I usually would reply that we weren't going to spend that much, or that a particular choice was too unhealthy. After tiring of the battles about whether to order the side items or whether to order water instead of soft drinks, I was inspired (divinely, I think) with this idea.

While on vacation, we stopped at one of those convenience gas stations with several fast-food chain restaurants inside. I just said, "We're going to do this differently today. I'm giving you $4 to buy what you want for lunch." The kids loved the idea. They had the opportunity to engage in a basic economic transaction and to make their own choices.

They made acceptable picks. I was relieved of the role of judge and arbiter. I'd taken away their opportunity to complain about my choice for them.

Such newfound independence teaches other lessons, too. On one occasion, our older daughter noticed the restaurant had given her onions on a sandwich when she'd specifically requested none. Rather than addressing the restaurant workers myself, I instructed her (an example of "as you go" training) on the importance of bringing this feedback politely to the management's attention. She was the customer; she gave a specific order; they should make it right. It was her first opportunity as a consumer to give such feedback. She had a good experience as employees gave her a new sandwich and profusely apologized.

Going Deeper:
If you want to learn more about how your kids respond, give them incentives to come back with change. Say, "Here's $5 for your lunch. If you come back with any change, we'll split it. You keep half and I'll keep half."

The amounts are up to you. The important—and interesting—thing is to learn more about your child's financial personality.

Compare Product Labels

Teaching Goals:
- To understand labels and the value offered by private brands.
- To see that products with the same ingredients have different prices.

Teaching Method:
- Parents ⇨ Intentional ⇨ As You Go

Age Range: 8-14
Sweet Spot Age Range: 9-12

Activity Description:
During your next trip to the grocery store, have your children help you select two brands of the same product. The products should have identical ingredients but a significant price difference. We suggest an item kids are familiar with, such as vitamin supplements, children's cold medicines, ketchup, peanut butter, or maple syrup.

Find and hold up the most popular name brand. Show your children the label listing ingredients. Explain that rules require product makers to reveal the ingredients of products that we put in or on our bodies. The first item in the ingredient list is the one used the most in the product. The second item is the one with the second highest concentration, and so on.

Then find and hold up the store brand or generic version of the product. Compare the ingredients and their order. If applicable, also compare the nutritional information. Compare the prices of the two products.

Ask your kids which you should buy. If they choose the lower priced item, congratulate your sharp shoppers. If they choose the higher priced item, ask why. Are they still influenced by advertising? If so, you can try the "Advertising Detectives" activity in this chapter. If they only shrug and respond, "It's not that big a difference," try giving them an incentive to save that money.

One way to do that is by celebrating the "found" savings. Buy some ice cream or a small toy with the difference you saved. This will help the lesson stick. (You may have more savings to celebrate with if you compare higher-priced products, such as vitamin supplements instead of lip balm.) After the treat, explain that you can't buy ice cream every time you buy vitamins—but you'll use the savings to help the family in other ways, such as paying for your house, saving to take a vacation, or buying Christmas gifts.

Background Information:

One of the blessings of my life is that I (Jeremy) rarely have to shop for our household needs. When my wife and daughter were both sick recently, however, I received the stereotypical call to pick up a couple of things on my way home from the office.

Stepping up to the challenge of a medical crisis in our home, I confidently ventured into the epicenter of social and economic life in small-town America: Wal-Mart. All I had to do was pick up cold medicine and toothpaste. How hard could that be? I could handle this—especially because there was no emergency request for feminine hygiene products.

Finding the toothpaste aisle, I recognized some familiar brands and began to grab one. Wait a minute! Did I want the tartar control, tartar protection, or total protection? *Hmm . . . whitening sounds good, too.* But did I want the dual action whitening or the whitening gels? Some of the whitening also added tartar control. Now, this was starting to get confusing. Besides just toothpaste, I could get toothpaste with baking soda, peroxide, antibacterial agents, and even mouthwash. That's right—mouthwash in the toothpaste!

I saw toothpaste for sensitive gums and sensitive teeth. Did I want regular or mint—or cinnamon rush, refreshing vanilla, or even chocolate hazelnut? (Chocolate? How can that be?) After picking a type of toothpaste, I faced another whole set of decisions: packaging. Did I want a pump? A family size or regular size tube? An unscrewing top or a flip-open top?

If an educated, financially sophisticated adult can be overwhelmed by a simple consumer transaction, think how confusing it is for kids. Trying to sort things out, I later searched the Internet. Believe it or not, I found a Web site devoted to toothpaste! It gave me insight to cut through the clutter:

> Most experts would agree that as long as your toothpaste
> contains fluoride, the brand you buy really doesn't matter.
> All toothpastes with fluoride work effectively to fight
> plaque and cavities. Of course, they also clean and polish
> tooth enamel. In addition, your toothpaste should bear the
> American Dental Association (ADA) seal of approval on
> the container, which means that adequate evidence of safety
> and efficacy have been demonstrated in clinical trials.[2]

So, most toothpastes are equally effective if they have the seal of approval. The rest is just marketing hyperbole and novelty.

On that shopping adventure, I found the children's cold medicines to present just as many choices. Wising up a bit, I started comparing labels. Most of the heavily advertised, cleverly packaged brand names had the same ingredients as the generic or private label. Of course, the prices were much higher for the brand names.

Make the superstore a learning lab. Your children can learn these basic, sharp-shopping principles from you in a matter of minutes.

Going Deeper:
With the help of your kids, find an example in your household where you've consciously chosen the name brand product over the private label (for better taste, nutrition, texture to use in a recipe, etc.). Make sure you've tried both brands and aren't unduly influenced by habit or advertising.

Explain that in some cases you may choose the higher-priced product for specific reasons. It's important for your children to know that a sharp shopper doesn't always automatically choose the lowest price. Sharp shoppers choose the best blend of quality and value. If no one will take the lowest-priced vitamin supplements because they taste horrible, then your family isn't reaching the objective of improving nutrition. Smart shoppers should assume the lowest price is the best value unless they find out differently from experience or independent reviews.

Acquaint your older children with independent consumer agencies and rating services, such as *Consumer Reports*. Refer to a copy of the magazine at the library or use the Web sites. Search the Internet with your kids to obtain reviews and consumer opinions for major purchases.

Be careful about organizations that endorse products and receive advertising from their manufacturers (popular magazines, for example, or certain Web sites). Show how some sites are really sponsored by the company owning the brand, though the company name may not appear there. Search a variety of independent sites before making a spending decision.

Conduct a Taste Test

Teaching Goal:
- To discern the quality and price differences between leading brands and less expensive brands.

Teaching Method:
Parents ⇨ Intentional ⇨ Created

Age Range: 4-10

Sweet Spot Age Range: 5-8

Activity Description:
Next time you're at the market, buy the leading name brand of a product and the competing generic product or private store brand. Make sure the products are comparable. For example, if you're taste-testing canned peaches, select fruit cut the same way and packed in the same type of syrup (light or heavy).

Have the whole family participate in a blindfolded taste test. In addition to blindfolding the participants, cover the label or otherwise disguise the products to prevent peeking. Taste tests work best on an empty stomach and when you eat a cracker or drink water between samples.

Let each person choose and explain his or her preference. If you want to go more in-depth, develop a list of criteria applicable to the product chosen: Which is crispier? What texture is better? Which is juicier, softer, smoother, etc.?

Tabulate the results. Then reveal your family's preferred product and its price.

Discuss how you might apply this information. If the less expensive product was chosen, then it's a no-brainer to begin purchasing that one. If it's a tie or very close, then the less expensive product is likely the best choice for overall value of price and quality. If the more expensive product is the winner by far, discuss how it may be worth the extra cost.

Background Information:
You can combine this project with the "Compare Product Labels" activity or relate it to the "Advertising Detectives" activity presented earlier in this chapter.

Going Deeper:
With older children, discuss that while quality is important, the "best" product may be overkill for the need. For example, you might taste-test chocolate. Let's say you compare an imported Swiss chocolate bar from an exclusive candy store with a Hershey's bar from the grocery store. Your family clearly decides that the Swiss bar is better in every respect. But it costs five times as much.

If you have a desire for something sweet, a Hershey's bar will satisfy it. Even though the Swiss bar is much better in quality, the cheaper bar satisfies the need. If the need is to impress a spouse with a Valentine's Day gift, of course, you might choose differently.

In the same way, it may be clear from every independent reviewer that a Mercedes is better than a Chevrolet. But that doesn't mean you can afford it. The Chevy may still meet your transportation need.

This activity should not give your kids the impression that the best quality is always the best choice. Older children can make this distinction. The best quality may not be within your means. Lower-quality, less expensive products may still fill the bill, providing better value for your money.

Brainstorming before Buying

Teaching Goals:
- To offer alternatives to buying.
- To help children think of creative ways to meet needs.

Teaching Method:
  • Parents ⇨ Intentional ⇨ As You Go
Age Range: 7-15
Sweet Spot Age Range: 10-13

Activity Description:
How many times have you toted your kids to the grocery store and mall? Ever since they were babies in a carrier, they probably have seen you buy things. When they need or want something, it's only natural for them to grab it off the shelf.

During your next shopping trip, help your child brainstorm alternatives to buying. For example, let's say that Nicole wants to buy a DVD, and let's assume it's a movie you approve of her seeing. Simply ask her, "What are some other ways you can satisfy your desire to see this movie without buying it?"

She may assume this is a ploy, a trick question, or an indication that you've already decided to say no to the purchase. So you may have to word your question more creatively: "Say you were on a game show. To win a fabulous vacation, you have to answer in 30 seconds this bonus question: Name three ways you could see this video without buying it today. Go."

Possibilities include the following:
  • Rent it.
  • Borrow it from a friend who has it.
  • Check it out of the library.
  • Buy it at a used CD/DVD store.
  • Ask for it as a birthday or Christmas gift.

These are the easier answers. You might keep challenging her to come up with more—even if they're off-the-wall. "Come on, what are some other legal ways you could see this video?"

  • Form a neighborhood exchange program that lets you pool videos and "check them out" for a period of time.
  • Buy it used from someone selling it on eBay or other Internet sites.

• See it at a "dollar" theater, matinee, or drive-in that shows older movies.
• Go to a place where TVs are sold and ask the manager to show it on the sets displayed (be ready to stand for a while!).
• Watch the TV listings to see if it will be on anytime soon.

Background Information:
The purpose of this activity is to awaken your child to alternatives. Even if you still buy the item in question, you've shown your child the possibility of alternatives and have given her an escape from the binary trap of decision making ("Should I buy this or not?") as discussed in Chapter 5.

Treasure Hunt for Change

Teaching Goal:
• To understand denominations of coins and their value.
Teaching Method:
• Parents ➪ Intentional ➪ Created
Age Range: 3-8
Sweet Spot Age Range: 4-6

Activity Description:
Announce that you and your children are going on a hunt for treasure. Explain that in your home, there are lost coins. Use any treasure-hunting garb and equipment (explorer hat, flashlights, etc.) you can find, and make a map with a layout of rooms and where lost coins may be.

Search in those places for spare change. Look under couch cushions, in the pockets of jackets and coats, under car seats and in glove compartments, in closets, around the washer and dryer, and in the bottoms of drawers. (If your house is spic-and-span and you don't think there are many coins to be found, place some under furniture in advance.) Be sure kids understand that they aren't allowed to take treasure that isn't lost—from a sibling's piggy bank or a parent's wallet or purse, for instance. Gather your treasure on a table. Ask your child to sort coins into separate piles—pennies in one, nickels in another, etc. Take one coin from each pile. Place one of the coins under a piece of white paper. Show your child how to slant a pencil and shade the area above the coin to reveal its image. Do this for each type of coin.

Under each image, you or your child should write the coin's common name (dime, quarter, pound, euro, etc.). Explain that each coin is worth a different amount. Write or ask your child to write how much each is worth.

Add up the value of the treasure. If your child can understand the math, have him or her total the amount. If he or she needs help, count it out loud together.

Reward your child for the found treasure. You might go out for a special treat or split the money between you. With your child's portion, consider using the "Give It, Save It, Spend It" activity in Chapter 9.

Background Information:
Counting is the first step to understanding currency and participating in your country's economy. To count, your child must understand how much each coin or paper currency represents. This activity can be repeated every few months for younger children as needed to reinforce what they've learned.

Going Deeper:
Read Jesus' short parable of the lost coin in Luke 15:8-10. Reminisce with your child about any time he was lost, even if only briefly. Ask your child how being lost felt. Then, recall how happy you both were when he was found.

Emphasize that your child should be careful with his coins and not lose them. Then go deeper with the theme of lostness, describing as simply as possible how we are spiritually "lost." God searches for us, pursues us, and celebrates when He finds us.

Coin Combo Platter Game

Teaching Goal:
   • To understand what coins are worth and improve counting abilities.
Teaching Method:
   • Parents ⇨ Intentional ⇨ Created
Age Range: 5-10
Sweet Spot Age Range: 6-8

Activity Description:
On your next trip to the bank (or the family change jar), obtain coins in at least the following amounts: 16 quarters, 50 dimes, 40 nickels, 100 pennies, and 4 half-dollars. Also, have a one-dollar bill available. (Note: Adapt the currency to fit your country as needed.)

Spread the change on a table and mix up the coins. You may need to review with your children what each is worth. Test kids by holding up a coin and asking its name and value.

Tell children that the object of this game is to choose the coins that add up to one dollar (or a comparable amount in your nation's currency). As in the Olympics, there will be three levels of winners. (If your children aren't familiar with the Olympic medal analogy, use another with three levels, such as intermediate, advanced, expert.) To win the bronze medal, they must combine only one type of coin to total one dollar (e.g., 4 quarters or 20 nickels). Players must add up all five possibilities to win.

To win the silver medal, they must add up coins totaling one dollar using 10 combinations of different coins. For example, they can't use four quarters to reach a dollar, but they can use two quarters and five dimes. To help them see all the combinations, have children leave each grouping on the table. This may seem difficult at first, but most children will soon see it's possible. There are nine combinations for dimes and nickels alone.

If kids advance past the second round, mix all the coins together again. To win the gold medal, they must use 20 combinations—without using any pennies. At this level, there will not be enough coins of each denomination to leave all the groupings out at once. You'll have to tally periodically the number of correct combinations and mix the coins up again to have enough.

Reward your children based on the level reached. You may wish to go out for a treat or divide some or all of the money.

Background Information:
The inspiration for this activity occurred when I (Jeremy) recently watched a young girl in a checkout lane. After placing her purchase on the counter, she gave the cashier far too much money. In this instance the cashier was gracious—and honest—enough to tell the girl she'd handed over too much. The cashier counted the correct change and returned the extra money.

In a world with many dishonest people looking to take advantage of the naïve, your children need to have basic money skills to survive. This "Combo Platter" can help.

Going Deeper:
As you review the piles of coins adding up to the same amount, pull out your dollar bill (or comparable currency). Point out that the bill is worth the same as each pile. Explain that all the piles are worth the same regardless of how many coins are in them. Younger kids sometimes have a hard time understanding that more coins don't necessarily mean more value.

Read the following Bible verse: *"Watch out! Be on your guard against all kinds of greed; a man's life does not consist in the abundance of his possessions"* (Luke 12:15). Focus on the latter part of this verse to suggest a broader lesson. He who has the most toys does not win. Many adults think that if they have more things, their lives are better. Point out that having more coins, or more things, doesn't mean a fuller, more meaningful life.

After completing this activity once, you might repeat it on other occasions with variations. Try different combinations of coins, or have them add up to a different total. You could stage a competition among siblings based on speed and the most combinations achieved—after applying the necessary adjustments or handicaps for different ages.

Trust...but Cut the Cards

Teaching Goals:
  • To learn to count the correct change.
  • To begin the habit of verifying change received.
Teaching Method:
  • Parents ⇨ Intentional ⇨ Created
Age Range: 5-10
Sweet Spot Age Range: 6-8

Activity Description:
Have your children set up a make-believe toy store. They can arrange their toys for display and think of a name for their store. You'll shop, and they'll be the cashiers. Explain that the store is just for pretending; they won't really sell or get rid of the toys permanently. And you'll get back the money you "spent."

Have kids put prices on the toys between $1.00 and $2.50 (adapt these amounts and others in this activity to your country's currency as needed). Encourage them to price items with cents, such as $1.75 or $1.90.

Provide one $5 bill, about seven $1 bills, and a few of each type of coin.

Shop for one item. Then go to "check out." Hand your children a $5 bill and have them practice giving the correct change. Let them watch you standing there, counting your change. Explain that this is an important habit to practice at stores.

Come back and shop again. Purchase several items to give your children practice adding up the total. Have them give change and then count it.

Switch roles and have your children be customers while you play cashier. Make sure they count the change at the counter before leaving.

Keep your children on their toes by giving them incorrect change to see if they notice. You also might try purchasing more than $5 worth of items and asking your kids to tell you what should be returned.

Background Information:
Former CBS news anchor Dan Rather said, "I trust my mother, but we cut the cards." Or as President Ronald Reagan put it, "Trust, but verify." Counting change is wise and prudent. We don't want to teach that people are untrustworthy, but that mistakes can happen—and we should help each other verify the correctness of our transactions.

Learning to count change helps children begin a "verifying habit." This habit eventually manifests itself in more advanced forms—like reading contracts before signing and reconciling bank accounts.

Read Sharp Shopping Books and Watch a Video

Teaching Goal:
  • To motivate your children in an entertaining way to be sharp shoppers.

Teaching Method:
Their Own Experience ⇨ Others
Age Range: Various

Activity Description:
Reading consumer guides and penny-pinching newsletters aren't nearly as interesting as the following reinforcements for your teaching. Decide which are most appropriate for your children.

Title: *The Berenstain Bears Get the Gimmes*
Author: Jan and Stan Berenstain (Random House, 1983)
Description: Can Mama and Papa Bear find a way to keep the cubs from begging at the store? In this colorful picture book, the famous bears face the challenges parents often do and work to convince their children they don't need it all.
Length: 35 pages
Age Range: 4-9

Title: *A Bargain for Frances*
Author: Russell Hoban (Harper Collins, 1970)
Description: Frances saves and saves for a china tea set. Her friend Thelma tricks her into buying an old plastic one. Thelma says there are no "backsies" on the bargain. Frances finds a way to get what she really wants.
Length: 62 pages
Age Range: 5-9

Title: VeggieTales: *Madame Blueberry* (video)
Author: Big Idea Productions, 1998
Description: Why is Madame Blueberry so blue? Because she wants more stuff. She has everything she needs, but some of her friends have a lot more. Sound familiar? Kids will learn that "being greedy makes you grumpy—but a thankful heart is a happy heart."

Length: 35 minutes
Age Range: 3-12

Title: *Alexander, Who Used to be Rich Last Sunday*
Author: Judith Viorst (Athenium, 1978)
Description: Alexander starts the week as a rich young man. Then the money begins to slip away. In the process, he learns that there are so many things that can be done with a dollar.
Length: 28 pages
Age Range: 5-10

Savvy Savers

From a Child's Perspective:
"A penny saved is . . . not much."—WILL, AGE 7

Bankers from American Trust in Dubuque, Iowa, acted as guest speakers in the local grade schools. They asked grade school students, "What would you like to save money for?" The more eyebrow-raising responses included the following:
- Money for a boyfriend and college
- A puppy
- My country
- A Harley-Davidson
- A Hummer limousine. When the boy who gave this answer was asked if he would be driving his friends around in it, he said, "No, but my butler would."

Biblical Principles:
In the house of the wise are stores of choice food and oil, but a foolish man devours all he has.—PROVERBS 21:20

"Let Pharaoh appoint commissioners over the land to take a fifth of the harvest of Egypt during the seven years of abundance. They should collect all the food of these good years that are coming and store up the

grain under the authority of Pharaoh, to be kept in the cities for food. This food should be held in reserve for the country, to be used during the seven years of famine that will come upon Egypt, so that the country may not be ruined by the famine."—GENESIS 41:34-36

Piggy Banking

Teaching Goals:
- To generate interest in saving.
- To point out the importance of dividing funds into saving, spending, and giving categories.

Teaching Method:
- Children ⇨ Their Own Money ⇨ Intentional

Age Range: 3-10

Sweet Spot Age Range: 4-7

Activity Description:

Remember those heavy piggy banks that were easy to put money into but difficult to open? Did you have a pink-colored pig that gave no indication of how much money you had?

You can do better with your child. Here are some new and improved "piggy banks" that aren't always swine related. (Availability and prices are subject to change.)

1. Crown Financial Ministries (www.crown.org) offers My Giving Bank. It's a three-compartment unit made of transparent blue plastic. Reminiscent of a city block, it has a picture of a bank for the saving compartment, a church for the giving compartment, and a store for the spending compartment. Crown Financial Ministries also includes free, Bible-based information for parents. Priced at $18.

2. Prosperity4kids, Inc. (www.prosperity4kids.com) developed the Money Mama Piggy Bank to give children a hands-on way to practice money management. It has four slots with their own

compartments to emphasize the 10/10/10/70 model for money received: give 10 percent to a charity of the child's choice, invest 10 percent to build his or her fortunes, save 10 percent for the future, and spend 70 percent for everyday expenses. The Mama Pig is the 70 percent spending category. In front of her stand the three little pigs of equal height (the three 10 percent categories). Made of ceramic, it costs $29.95.

3. Similar to #2, but less expensive at $14.99, is the Money Savvy Pig. Sold by Money Savvy Generation (www.msgen.com), it has four chambers for "Save," "Spend," "Donate," and "Invest." It also has an easy-to-access slot to add dollars and coins. The Money Savvy Pig is made of translucent plastic, so children can easily see how much is accumulating. A Moolah Cow Bank is available for the same price.

4. Piggybankworld.com offers all kinds of coin saving devices, personalized banks, banks in the shape of other animals, "dinosaur belly banks," safes, mechanical coin banks, musical banks, and more pigs than you've probably ever cared to see.

Background Information:

Did you ever wonder how a pig became associated with saving?

The true history of the piggy bank is somewhat uncertain. But there appears to be a consensus that it derives its name from the orange clay, "pygg," from which it was originally made. During the Middle Ages, metal was expensive and hard to find in Europe. Families used inexpensive "pygg" clay to create household pots and jars.

In England, coins were kept in such jars. The so-called "pig" jar retained its name long after potters stopped using "pygg" clay to produce pottery. By the turn of the eighteenth century, the jars had acquired the name of "pig banks," from which followed "piggy bank." These banks were ceramic and had no hole in the bottom, so the pig had to be broken to get the money out.

A variation of this history is that younger or foreign craftsmen were frequently asked to create pygg banks. Misunderstanding the request, the potters crafted banks in the shape of pigs and painted them accordingly.

Another theory is that the piggy bank acquired its name because in some ways it's treated like a real pig. The bank is "fed" the scraps and leftovers of one's small change until it's fat enough to be smashed and the savings retrieved.

To this day in some European nations, notably the Netherlands and German-speaking countries, it's customary to give piggy banks as gifts because pigs are thought to bring good fortune. On New Year's Day, so-called "Lucky Pigs" are still exchanged as gifts. Children are given piggy banks as birthday or Christmas presents to encourage saving. Major banks have often given piggy banks to children in an attempt to do the same.[1]

Picture Your Savings Goal

Teaching Goals:
   • To set savings goals.
   • To provide motivation for delaying gratification.
Teaching Method:
   • Children ⇨ Their Own Money ⇨ As You Go
Age Range: 6-12
Sweet Spot Age Range: 8-11

Activity Description:
Has your child ever begged you to buy the latest toy or doll or electronic gizmo? Being the wise parent you are, you likely responded with, "Well, start saving your own money."

Let's follow up on that comment by helping your child set a goal and then using visual reminders to achieve that goal.

Help your child find a picture of the item she desires to save for. From magazines, Web sites, catalogs, ad circulars, or newspaper ads, choose a good picture and cut it out.

Place the picture in a prominent place where she keeps her money or where it will be seen often. For younger children, tape the picture to a piggy bank. For older ones, put it on a bulletin board, mirror, or in a purse. Be creative in monitoring progress. Consider drawing a thermometer on a small poster. Have your child color in the thermometer to show how she's doing in reaching her goal.

Background Information:
Delayed gratification is an important character trait for financial maturity. But there should be some eventual gratification. The hoarders among us tend toward saving just for saving's sake. This can be discouraging to a child.

In the White family, we had successfully used the "Give Some, Save Some, Spend Some" activity (see Chapter 9) for over a year. We regularly divided incoming money into the categories of giving, spending, and savings. My younger daughter astutely asked me one day, "What's the purpose of the savings category? What are we saving for?"

I stammered, "Well, that's for emergencies. It's for stuff you want to buy or things you want to do later." Knowing my reply didn't create a groundswell of enthusiasm and motivation, I've used this more concrete activity to provide the tangible reminder that money is a tool to help us reach our objectives.

Saving money is a difficult discipline, even for adults and governments! But, establishing a savings habit is important. To keep a balanced view, however, the savings should have a target.

Kids don't need emergency reserves like parents do. They don't have roofs to replace, transmissions that go out, layoffs to deal with, or semi-annual insurance to pay. Your child's savings can be allocated—some for college, some for summer camp, some for an MP3 player, and so on. He or she may have some savings goals that are simply not identified yet—perhaps for a future concert or a youth group trip.

Family 401(k)

Teaching Goals:
- To begin the habit of regular saving and investing in a format similar to the popular 401(k) retirement plan.
- To set up longer-term savings and specify in advance the conditions for withdrawals.

Teaching Method:
- Parents ⇨ Intentional ⇨ Created

Age Range: 10-18
Sweet Spot Age Range: 13-16

Activity Description:

Set up a "Family 401(k)" to encourage saving for specific purposes. (Note: This not an actual 401(k) or retirement plan. There is no government filing or IRS approval required, and no tax benefits.) Simply announce to your kids at your next family gathering that you're going to reward them for saving.

First, tell them the big picture. For every dollar they save toward a specific purpose (college, for example), you'll make a matching contribution. To get the match, they'll need to follow some rules.

Before the meeting, you and your spouse should discuss and agree on the rules of your plan by asking yourselves the following questions:

1. What will be your matching contribution? For example, you could choose a 100 percent, or-dollar-for dollar, match. (We recommend this as a straightforward approach.) Or, you could match 50 cents on the dollar, or even $3 for every dollar saved.

2. Will there be a limit to the amount of your matching contribution? Because most employers have a limit and because you want to fulfill your obligation, you may wish to set one. That hoarding-prone child may wreak havoc on your savings otherwise!

For example, you might consider a maximum dollar limit, such as $500.

3. What are the conditions under which money can be withdrawn without a penalty? In other words, what are the specific purposes for this long-term savings? You may define it as an education fund for college or post-secondary technical school. You might say it's a car fund. Choose longer-term, higher-dollar items rather than a bicycle or video game. (We have another savings incentive for these lower-cost items. See the "Matching Short-Term Savings Goals" activity later in this chapter.) Perhaps a honeymoon fund, mission trip, or down payment fund for a first house are other choices.

4. What is the penalty if money is withdrawn for other purposes? We suggest you impose a rather stiff monetary penalty if withdrawals occur for purposes other than the ones you've identified. Let's say your Family 401(k) is to be used for either higher education or a mission trip. But David, Jr. wants to use it for a car. You could impose a penalty of 50 percent of your matching contribution, or even 100 percent of the match. You may wish to prohibit certain transactions altogether, though this gets tougher as the child gets older.

5. Where will the account be held and how will it be registered? Initially, it may be easier to have a savings account at a local bank. As more money accumulates, consider investing in mutual funds. Many mutual funds have minimum account opening balances as low as $250 or $500. You could hold the funds in your name only or in a custodial account (UGMA/UTMA—Uniform Gift to Minors Act or Uniform Transfer to Minors Act). Or, you may wish to use a tax-advantaged college-savings account if you are limiting the use to education.

We recommend that you actually write up and sign a "plan document." This will also give your kids practice at reading contracts, asking questions, and making commitments.

Background Information:
Named after section 401(k) of the Internal Revenue Code, company-sponsored 401(k) plans are the most common retirement plans used in the workplace today. Many not-for-profit entities have similar arrangements called 403(b) plans, named after another tax code section. Small businesses and sole proprietorships may offer other types of plans. For simplicity, we'll refer to all retirement plans under the general name of 401(k).

These plans are designed to offer tax benefits today to entice people to save for their own retirement. Many employers prefer these retirement plans over traditional pension plans because the amount of the contribution is defined without obligating the employer to guarantee specific results from the investment.

If employees set aside money from their paychecks, the employer matches the employee's contribution up to a certain percentage. Employees can choose how to invest their money and usually how to invest the employer's contribution.

The 401(k) plans in the workplace are designed for long-term savings, usually retirement. Generally, employees cannot access the money. If they do before age 59½, there is a price to pay: a 10 percent penalty. In addition, they must pay income tax on the amount withdrawn.

If your children can have a positive experience with your Family 401(k), they're likely to save early and significantly in a future employer's 401(k) plans.

Explain to your kids that most people save for retirement through similar arrangements. If you're saving in a 401(k), show them some of the literature or summary descriptions provided by your employer.

Going Deeper:
This activity can develop into another that teaches selecting and investing in mutual funds. If you're knowledgeable about mutual funds, explain their purpose to your kids. Select a quality fund that

you're familiar with and set up an account. Your financial adviser probably can help you with this specific-purpose account for your children.

"Let's Make a Money Deal" Game Show

Teaching Goals:
- To illustrate the powerful effects of compounding interest over time.
- To sharpen math skills.

Teaching Method:
- Parents ➪ Intentional ➪ As you go

Age Range: 10-18

Sweet Spot Age Range: 11-14

Activity Description:

On your next long drive, right after the snacks run out and before your children ask, "Are we there yet?" try this activity.

Say to your kids, "Let's pretend you're on a game show. You've made it to the final round. If you answer just one more question correctly, you win one of two fabulous cash prizes."

Ask a math question that you're fairly certain your kids will get right. Depending on their age, it might be "What is the square root of 64?" or "How many large pizzas, cut into 8 slices, would it take to allow 12 people at a party to eat two slices each?" You can make up most any question; the question isn't as important as what's coming next.

Congratulate your kids on being math whizzes. They win the grand prize of lots of money!

They have two choices of how to receive their grand prize. Due to the show's tight schedule, they only have 15 seconds to decide between them. Choice A is receiving $50,000 per day for

31 days. Choice B is receiving the result of a penny doubled every day for 31 days.

In other words, Choice A is receiving $50,000 on day 1, another $50,0000 on day 2, another $50,000 on day 3, and so on. After four days, your kids would have $200,000 under Choice A.

Choice B brings them a penny after day one, two cents after day 2, four cents after day 3, eight cents after day 4, 16 cents after day 5, and so on. After five days, they have 16 cents (not the sum of one cent, two cents, four cents, etc.).

Don't give them time to compute the totals before they respond. After explaining the options, stick to the 15-second time limit and ask for their final choice. After making their decision, they can't change their minds.

Then have them compute the total amount of both choices to see if they made the best decision. (This is where you can pass some time on the road and sharpen their math skills a bit.) The $50,000 is fairly easy. The answer is the cumulative total $1,550,000.

The doubling of the penny will take some time to compute. The answer is a whopping $10,737,418!

Talk about the results. Were kids surprised? How long did it take Choice B to overtake Choice A? Why did they choose their option?

Point out that choosing Choice A was a $9 million mistake. That should be some incentive to pay closer attention in math class!

Background Information:
In your discussion, point out the patience required to realize the value of the power of compounding. The game is decided in the fourth quarter. It was day 29 when Choice B overtook Choice A, but those final days made all the difference. Similarly, the small bits of interest added to a savings account may not seem like much at first. Over time, however, the little bits turn into big bits.

Choice B in this activity assumed a rate of return of 100 percent per day. This is an impossible rate to find in a financial investment. (You should run away from anyone who promises you such a rate!) We used an unreasonable rate to focus on the powerful effects of compounding over time.

Going Deeper:
Children may have a difficult time understanding the concept of compounding. Indeed, adults have a hard time grasping its power. Albert Einstein is reported to have said, "Compounding is the greatest discovery in the twentieth century."

To help your children understand the idea of earning interest on top of interest or return on top of return, explain that compounding is like multiplying instead of adding. Have them write on a piece of paper two rows of five 2's separated by a space:

2   2   2   2   2
2   2   2   2   2

In the first row, ask your child to insert the "+" sign between the numbers and add up the total. Then, for the second row, insert the "x" sign for multiplication and compute the result.

2 + 2 + 2 + 2 + 2 = 10
2 x 2 x 2 x 2 x 2 = 32

Explain further by pretending your children have $100 in their savings accounts. If the interest rate is 5 percent, use simple interest (like adding) to compute the balance 10 years from today. The answer is $150 because you're adding $5, or 5 percent, per year.

If your child receives compounded interested (like multiplying), the balance in 10 years would be $162.89. After the first year, the balance is the same as simple interest, $105. But in the second year, your child's balance would be $105 times 5 percent, or $110.25.

Opportunity Knocks

Teaching Goal:
  • To illustrate the opportunity cost of consuming today instead of saving.

Teaching Method:
  • Parents ⇨ Intentional ⇨ As you go
Age Range: 12-18
Sweet Spot Age Range: 13-16

Activity Description:
Identify an item that your children tend to waste money on. Think of temptations that get the best of them: the daily ice cream, her fifteenth shade of lip gloss, his video games, her chocolate.

Ask how much the item costs.

Say, "That's how much it costs *today*. But what does it cost in terms of what you're giving up?"

They may grunt, "Huh?" and think this is just another parental trick question. And it is.

Help kids compute an average annual amount spent on their luxury. Let's say they spend $2 per day, 4 days a week. That's $416 per year ($2 times 4 days times 52 weeks). An estimate is fine; guess on the high side.

Now compare the estimate to the alternative of saving that money. Let's say your children buy a $2 treat just once a week instead. They save the rest—which comes to $312 ($2 times 3 days times 52 weeks per year). Saving that money for 40 years at a 5 percent interest rate will result in over $39,500! That's some expensive ice cream!

Be sure to point out that only $12,480 ($312 times 40 years) was actually saved. The other $27,020 was from the effect of compounding. Compounding simply means earning interest on top of interest.

Background Information:
When checking out of a drugstore or a supermarket, have you ever bought a magazine, candy bar, or something else on impulse? We've all fallen prey to that temptation, and retailers know this.

"Opportunity Knocks" has a dual purpose. It gives incentive to stop overspending in a certain area and provides motivation to save. Let's see how it might work on you.

Let's say, on the average, you impulsively spend $3.75 a day on candy, newspapers, soft drinks, and other little items. If you do that every year for 50 years, you will have forked over $68,000. But the real cost of those impulse purchases isn't the $3.75 a day; it's what you *could* have done with those discretionary dollars.

If you'd invested $1,368 ($3.75 times 365 days) per year in an IRA (Individual Retirement Account), 50 years later you'd have more than $300,000 if you earned 5 percent interest per year. In other words, choosing to spend the $3.75 a day cost you what you *could* have earned—$300,000. This is the opportunity cost of consumption.

Going Deeper:
Computing the long-term effects of compounding can be quite motivating to your children (and to you). Using a constant interest rate—say 5 percent—play with the calculator to figure out the following:

• If your children saved $1 per day for the next 10 years, how much would they have?
• At age 50, how much would your children have if they saved $1 per day for the next 40 years?
• How much would you have to save per month to have $1 million after 40 years?
• How much per day would it take to save this amount?

In the Intelligent Investors activities in Chapter 10, we'll focus on the significant difference the assumed interest rate (or rate of return) can make with the power of compounding.

Matching Short-Term Savings Goals

Teaching Goal:
• To provide incentives to help your child save for specific purposes.

Teaching Method:
    • Parents ⇨ Intentional ⇨ Created
Age Range: 6-16
Sweet Spot Age Range: 8-12

Activity Description:

After your child has set a goal to save for a specific item, you can announce your intention to match her savings. You may decide to match dollar for dollar or even three to one.

You might only want to do this for fairly costly items that you think would benefit your child. For example, you may have bought the first bicycle your child received. You thought it was worthwhile for him to learn to ride, to get some exercise, and to spend time with the family. Maybe you were just excited about watching your child take off!

But when he starts thinking about the latest edition of a "cool" bike, you might decide he needs to have some "skin in the game." Saving for a bike on a child's budget probably would take an unreasonable amount of time, so this activity might be a good choice.

Other possible short-term goals could include summer camp, a musical instrument, or a special trip with a youth group. Here are some "do's and don'ts" to keep in mind as you set up your matching program.
    • Do set an upper limit on your match.
    • Do be consistent with all children.
    • Don't match the first item the child saves for—she needs to have the sense of accomplishment of saving on her own.
    • Don't match every item the child is saving for—just selected ones.

Background Information:

Americans can be proud of many things, but not their savings habits. They're the worst savers among the industrialized countries of the world, coming in at less than 2 percent annually.[2] Regardless of the country in which you live, you need to do all you can to encourage the habit of saving.

Children can get discouraged easily by how long it takes to reach a goal. Waiting can build patience and reflects the real world—but the goal here is to help kids get in the habit of saving and being excited about it. Your time frame is so short that a matching program can boost their learning.

For older children, this matching approach can be used for more significant items—like a car, computer, or college tuition.

Play Math Computer Games

Teaching Goal:
  • To sharpen the basics of math skills in an entertaining way.
Teaching Method:
  • Children ⇨ Their Own Experience ⇨ Others
Age Range: 4-12, depending on the game
Sweet Spot Age Range: 7-10

Activity Description:
Success in basic math skills will help your children have a better chance of succeeding financially. They'll still have to show self-control and make good decisions, of course—even if their IQ is over 200.

Alan Greenspan, former Chairman of the Federal Reserve Bank and one of the most powerful influences on the U.S. economy, made the following observation:

> It has been my experience that competency in mathematics . . . enhances a person's ability to handle the more ambiguous and qualitative relationships that dominate our day-to-day financial decision making.[3]

Unfortunately, most every survey of educational ability reveals that children need improvement in math.

Because most children love computer games and usually don't like working math problems, here's a solution. Play educational games that reinforce math skills. Most players don't even realize they're learning.

Many Web sites offer free math games for kids. To find them, do an Internet search. Here are just a few sites in this category as we write this book:

www.homeschoolmath.net

www.dositey.com

www.aplusmath.com

www.coolmath4kids.com

www.10ticks.co.uk/games/asp

www.funbrain.com

As for computer math games you can buy, there are scores of choices. Search the Internet for descriptions and reviews of games like these:

The *Jumpstart* series from Knowledge Adventure

The *Math Blaster* series from Davidson and Associates

The *Reader Rabbit Math* series from the Learning Company

Math Missions: The Race to Spectacle City Arcade Grade K-2 and *Math Missions: The Amazing Arcade Adventure Grades 3-5* from Scholastic

Soccer Math from EdVenture Software

Money Town from Simon and Schuster Interactive

Dollarville from Waypoint Software

Coin Critters from Nordic Software

Millie's Math House from Edmark

Carmen Sandiego Math Detective from Broderbund

Background Information:

Having a quick mind with math facts and computation can help your child avoid being duped. It's amazing how a little calculation can help a youngster see through clever marketing or sales tactics. Recently we saw a sign for one of those check-cashing "stores." They advertised, "Get $200 today and only pay back $203 next week."

The not-so-swift fellow who thought math wouldn't apply to everyday life might say to himself, "Doesn't sound like a bad deal to me."

But your money-smart, math-sharp, savvy saver might do some quick calculation and say, "That's highway robbery! One and a half percent interest for one week is an annual interest rate of 78 percent!"

Doing endless worksheets may not be fun, but math is necessary. Try a few games to generate more interest and reinforce quick-thinking number skills.

Making Savings More "Interest"-ing

Teaching Goal:
• To illustrate the idea of earning interest.
Teaching Method:
• Parents ⇨ Intentional ⇨ Created
Age Range: 4-10
Sweet Spot Age Range: 5-7

Activity Description:

Suggest to your children that they open a "savings account" at home. Tell them you'll pay interest on the amount they keep in the "bank." Consider paying them monthly.

Refrain from talk of interest rates and percentages. Simply say this is a reward for savings. You can later use that language when your kids open bank accounts: "The bank is rewarding you for saving with it."

Make the amount you pay proportional to a child's savings

balance; that is, your contribution will increase or decrease as savings increase or decrease. Consider asking each child to tally his or her balance before you pay. Counting practice never hurts anyway.

Background Information:
Banks are often inconvenient for young savers. Though we recommend learning about the banking system at an early age, it's not always practical to open very small-balance accounts.

Most families are too busy to find time during banking hours to take their children there. Some banks have minimum opening balances for kids' accounts; others may have service fees. If an account is dormant (having no activity) for a period of time, it may be subject to a fee or even be temporarily closed.

This activity solves all these practical challenges. Perhaps more importantly, your children see the actual amount of interest earned. It's difficult for a younger child to appreciate the interest added on a quarterly statement.

My (Jeremy's) daughters have a small savings account at a bank. I was looking forward to teaching them about interest and how money grows. During the low-interest years of the early 2000s, their quarterly interest additions were a measly 16 cents!

Not only were they not impressed, but they also had a difficult time grasping what had happened. A benefit of this at-home activity is that your child receives, handles, and adds money to savings in more tangible and encouraging ways than at a local bank.

Read Savvy Saver Books

Teaching Goal:
 • To convince your child to be a regular saver.
Teaching Method:
 • Their Own Experience ⇨ Others
Age Range: Various

Activity Description:
Seeing the success of others saving money can be a powerful motivator. We all need a little nudge to save for future rewards. The following books will encourage the discipline of saving. For books marked with an asterisk (*), offer an "extra credit" incentive if your child writes a book report.

Title: *The Richest Man in Babylon**
Author: George Clason (Hawthorne Books, 1955)
Description: When providing debt counseling and financial advice to clients, I (Jeremy) require this as a homework assignment. This classic is a very readable story and provides some age-old secrets to managing money wisely. It poignantly describes the steps to do well financially—or to do horribly.
Length: 144 pages
Age Range: 12-18

Title: *The Riches of Oseola McCarty**
Author: Evelyn Coleman (Albert Whitman & Co., 1998)
Description: The true story of Oseola McCarty, an African-American woman in Mississippi, who worked all her life washing and ironing other people's clothes. She never earned more than $9,000 in one year, but made national headlines when she gave $150,000 to the University of Southern Mississippi at age 87. Find out how she did it through saving. This children's book, illustrated by Daniel Minter, tells the story of a woman who loved the Lord and loved to give.
Length: 48 pages
Age Range: 10-18

Title: *My Rows and Piles of Coins*
Author: Tololwa M. Mollel (Clarion Books, 1999)
Description: Saruni saves money he receives from helping his mother. His goal is to save enough money to buy a bicycle, so that

he can better help his mother carry food to the marketplace. He works and saves his money for a long time, only to have his hopes dashed. But in a surprise ending, his self-discipline and caring are rewarded.

Length: 31 pages
Age Range: 6-10

Title: *Money Trouble*
Author: Bill Cosby (Scholastic, 1998)
Description: Little Bill wants to become famous by discovering a new comet, but first he needs a telescope. The telescope he wants costs $100 and he only has $47.87 in his football bank. Little Bill finds ways to earn money through jobs.

Length: 36 pages
Age Range: 6-8

Prudent Planners

From a Child's Perspective:
You never know what's around life's corner, so eat your dessert first.—LECISHA, AGE 8

What are the personal qualities necessary to be a good marriage partner?
"One of you should know how to write a check. Because, even if you have tons of love, there is still going to be a lot of bills."
—AVA, AGE 8

Biblical Principles:
The plans of the diligent lead to profit as surely as haste leads to poverty.—PROVERBS 21:5

"Suppose one of you wants to build a tower. Will he not first sit down and estimate the cost to see if he has enough money to complete it? For if he lays the foundation and is not able to finish it, everyone who sees it will ridicule him, saying, 'This fellow began to build and was not able to finish.'"—LUKE 14:28-30

The prudent see danger and take refuge, but the simple keep going and suffer for it.—PROVERBS 27:12

Give Some, Save Some, Spend Some

Teaching Goal:
  • To develop the habit of dividing earnings among saving, giving, and spending.

Teaching Method:
  • Parents ⇨ Intentional ⇨ As you go

Age Range: 3-10

Sweet Spot Age Range: 4-7

Activity Description:

Establish the routine of dividing a child's incoming money evenly between giving, saving, and spending. Your earliest instruction should be simply, "When you receive money, you give some, save some, and spend some."

With young children, we suggest keeping it simple and allocating money evenly among the three categories. Though that's a high percentage to give, it's always easier to move the percentage down than up. The same is true with saving.

When giving your children allowances or paying for other work, try to make the amount easily divisible by three. For example, give them 75 cents with three quarters, or three dollars with one-dollar bills. Then they can easily divide the amount into three categories.

This activity is really an idea to use on a continuing basis. To develop this habit, you must help your kids allocate, then reinforce and remind. When new sources of income develop—cash gifts, contest prizes, earnings from extra jobs—work through this same allocation model.

Background Information:

From their earliest days of receiving money, our kids (the Whites) learned this method. It worked well at keeping straight the basic concepts of handling income. Wouldn't adults do much better by simply saying, "For every dollar I receive, I'll give some, save some, and spend some"?

Our kids had this habit ingrained in their thinking. As they were older, they automatically divided the proceeds. We even used this "asset allocation model" for monetary gifts received.

This activity is a good beginning step. As our children became older, we required them to track their spending (see the next activity, "Treasure Trackers"). Then we began using the envelope system described in Chapter 4.

The beauty of this activity is its simplicity. You're taking the complexity of personal finance and boiling it down into three memorable statements: give some, save some, spend some. This doesn't answer all questions or issues. But if a person does these three things consistently, he or she will do pretty well managing money.

~~~~~~~~~~~~~~

Treasure Trackers

Teaching Goal:
  • To develop the habit of tracking money and reconciling accounts.
Teaching Method:
  • Parents ➪ Intentional ➪ Created
Age Range: 5-9
Sweet Spot Age Range: 6-8

Activity Description:
Set one condition for receiving an allowance: Your kids have to track where their money goes.

Let's say they're dividing their allowances or gifts received into the three-category "Give Some, Save Some, Spend Some" model described in the previous activity. Set up an easy-to-follow accounting system:

- Obtain a one-inch, three-ring binder. Let kids decorate it or make a creative cover for their "money books."
- Insert in the binder three pencil/supply pouches that have the three holes pre-punched. Use these pouches to keep the bills and coins. (You could also use coin purses, a recipe box, chambered savings banks, or any other storage for the money.)
- Get three sheets of lined notebook paper with holes pre-punched. Label one "Savings," one "Spending," and one "Giving." Near the top of each sheet, put these headings:

  <u>Date</u>   <u>Description</u>   <u>Increase</u>   <u>Decrease</u>   <u>Amount Left</u>

- Explain to your children the object of this activity: The number in the "Amount Left" column must equal the amount of money in the pouch (or box or chamber or whatever). If it does, they receive their allowance. If not, they don't. You may choose to prorate the penalty if only one category is out of balance.
- Hold them accountable by double-checking their records and counting their money with them *before* you give them their new allowance.
- Consider reminding them a few minutes before you distribute their allowances to make sure they "balance" before you check.

Background Information:

Kids usually thrive on routines, knowing what's expected and feeling they have some control. This activity can help kids have pride in their accomplishments and feel like they truly manage their money. You may have to work with them for a few weeks before they're ready to keep track of money on their own.

When my (Jeremy's) daughters began receiving an allowance, I wanted them to begin the habit of tracking where their money went and reconciling. We set up their "money notebooks" in a three-ring binder. They decorated the outside of it. They felt they were "doing business paperwork" when they retrieved their money books. Every Sunday morning I gave them six dimes, which they could easily divide into their categories.

The threat of losing their allowance, or a portion of it, has provided enough motivation for our girls to "do their money books." If your child is still reluctant, consider offering a reward for correctly completing the balancing several weeks in a row.

Mention the words *budget*, *accounting*, or *reconciling*, then watch the facial muscles of most adults contort and contract. Almost invariably people think about constraints, inflexibility, rigidity, guilt, and other negative images. In reality, making a budget is the same as taking a trip with a pre-planned route. When you get to an intersection, you know which way to go. Rather than creating rigidity, a budget brings freedom. It lessens confusion, fear, and frustration.

Living without a short-term spending plan will inevitably lead to fear, frustration, confusion—and, in a marriage relationship, conflict. If lack of planning evokes these emotions in adults, imagine the effect it can have on a child trying to learn how to handle money.

Give your children financial freedom by teaching them the skill of budgeting. When they learn this skill and apply it, it will become a habit. Start with tracking; that leads to budgeting. It requires some of your time now. But it could save you, your spouse, and your children years of heartache, time, effort, and resources down the road.

When adults say they need to budget but appear overwhelmed, we tell them to start tracking expenditures first for a month or two. Don't budget yet, we say; just see where the money is going now.

What usually happens is something like this: "Hmm, honey. Last month, we spent $500 going out to eat. I had no idea it added up to that much."

"Me either," the spouse replies. "How about let's try to spend only $200 next month going out to eat?"

Voila! Budgeting just happened. Budgeting is simply deciding in advance where the money will go. But to have any reference point, you must see where you are now. When you begin tracking outgo, you can better direct it.

The Time-and-Money Coupon Gift

Teaching Goals:
- To illustrate the key element of financial planning: allocating limited financial resources among various unlimited alternatives.
- To give your kids experience planning and scheduling an event with a predetermined budget.

Teaching Method:
- Parents ⇨ Intentional ⇨ As you go

Age Range: 8-18
Sweet Spot Age Range: 10-16

Activity Description:
For Christmas, a birthday, or another special occasion, give your child an envelope with a special coupon. This coupon is worth four hours of your time and can be applied to any activity your child chooses. It's also worth $25 (or any other amount you deem appropriate) to spend on that activity.

Explain the conditions of use: Your child must take the initiative to make sure the date fits your schedule and to make any reservations or other plans—and can't get out of music lessons or chores to do it.

You may wish to offer a list of possibilities to start the creative juices, particularly for younger children. For example, you may suggest the following:
- Attend a local college ball game
- Go skating

- Go on a mall shopping spree and then to lunch
- Go camping
- Visit a ceramics studio and paint your own figurine or other item
- Buy and build a model together
- Attend a play
- Go to a concert
- Other: _____

Emphasize that your child gets to pick the activity and that the money has to pay for both of you.

Background Information:
Besides teaching how to plan and schedule, your objective is to let your child know she's important. You want to spend time one-to-one with her. You're letting her choose how she'd really like to spend time with you.

After one Christmas when I (Ron) gave our children this Time-and-Money Coupon, one of my daughters chose the option of spending four hours with me on a shopping spree. Nine years old, she carefully planned our time together. We were to start at a large shopping mall on a Saturday morning and end with lunch. She was filled with anticipation and excitement when the day arrived.

Picture in your mind a nine-year-old child with $25 in her hand, entering a mall that has tens of millions of dollars' worth of goods available to buy. The dilemma she faced is exactly the same dilemma you and I face—there's never enough money to do or buy everything you want. There are more ways to spend money than there is money available.

After shopping for a little while, we found ourselves in a store that offered overpriced notions like crazy pens, novelties, and note paper. She saw all the brightly colored, captivating items and responded to the urge that whispers, "Buy me! Buy me!"

"Honey," I cautioned, "remember that good decision making

requires a long-term perspective. Tomorrow these things will not be nearly so attractive."

With all the persuasive charm of a nine-year-old, she assured me she would use and love these items "forever and forever." When the clerk totaled the bill, she'd spent her $25—and we still had three hours left and lunch to buy. We ended up going home early so that she could play with her purchases.

The very next day, everything my daughter had purchased was either used up, broken, or uninteresting. I'll never forget her sheepishly admitting to me that she had, in effect, responded to the impulse of the moment and later realized she'd made a poor choice. The problem was that her money and time were both irretrievably lost.

What wasn't lost, however, was the experience and what it taught her. When she was older, she frequently reminded me when I was getting ready to buy something, "Daddy, don't forget that the more long-term your perspective, the better your decision is likely to be." Sometimes I wish I hadn't taught her that! Nevertheless, she learned as a nine-year-old four truths of financial planning that many adults never take to heart:

1. All of us have limited resources.

2. There are more options available than money.

3. Today's decisions determine destiny; a dollar spent is gone forever and can never be used in the future for anything else.

4. The more long-term the perspective, the better the potential for wise decisions.

When it comes to spending habits, most of us are responders rather than planners. We respond to friends, advertising, and emotions rather than looking ahead.

But when we know for certain what financial resources we have and plan to use them to accomplish God-given goals and objectives, we live in peace and contentment. We live in order instead of chaos. Frustration from overwhelming choices disappears. We're freed from the pressures of the short-term, self-gratifying society around us.

We're free to be different.

~~~~~~~~~~~

Birthday Date and Goal Setting

Teaching Goal:
- To guide your children in setting goals.

Teaching Method:
- Parents ⇨ Intentional ⇨ Created

Age Range: 8-18
Sweet Spot Age Range: 12-16

Activity Description:
Goal setting is important, but few of us feel an urgency about it. Our day-to-day activities tend to squeeze out long-term planning.

Because of this, we've found it helpful to set aside a specific time for goal setting. Many people think about this at the end of the year when making New Year's resolutions. That's fine, but we suggest each child's birthday as a more personalized time to discuss goals, beginning at age eight.

When that time rolls around, try an approach like the following.

Go out to a special restaurant—beyond the ordinary fast food, but something your child would enjoy.

Affirm and bless your child for progress made during the past year. Help him remember some accomplishments: learning to swim, writing in cursive, mastering multiplication tables, giving regularly, etc.

Ask your child what he'd like to accomplish during the coming year. You may have to help narrow down such an open question by dividing goals into categories: physical, friendships, savings, school, etc.

Write the goals in a special notebook and review them periodically.

Background Information:
In the Blue family, we parents took each child out for a special dinner on his or her birthday, just the three of us. During the meal we reviewed goals set the year before and whether or not they'd been accomplished.

Then we talked about goals the child would like to set for the next year and recorded them. This really helps children focus on activities in which they want to participate and to think about how God would have them use their time and talents.

Of course, there's nothing biblical or magical about the birthday date. But it's a special time for each child. Few parents and virtually no children ever forget birthdays. With five kids in the Blue family, it's been easy to treat children as a group rather than as individuals. This activity has allowed us to focus on each child as we discuss allowance, chores, and plans.

In some cases, we set goals during the year and posted them on the refrigerator so they could be seen on a regular basis. Examples would be practicing a sport for thirty minutes a day, reading two hours per week, or improving a grade in a difficult subject. Goals must be attainable. For example, the goal to shoot twelve thousand free throws per day, seven days a week, is not realistic. Allowing a child to set this type of goal will only cause frustration.

Three principles need to be applied when teaching your children goal setting:

1. Goals must be periodically reviewed. If they aren't, kids will forget them or have no positive feedback to encourage success.

2. If a goal is to be motivational, it must be recorded where your child can see it regularly.

3. The goal must be measurable, so that you know when it's been accomplished.

The goals you and your child set may not be as important as learning the *process* of setting them. We've encouraged our children to set goals in almost every area of life. Making friends, earning grades, saving, tithing, making major purchases, and being disciplined are areas in which our children have set goals. Besides helping them set goals, we've reviewed with them their successes and failures in pursuing those objectives.

One of the worst things we can imagine is raising children without helping them understand their purpose in life. Having goals helps them focus on that. How sad for people to reach the end of life and see how little they've accomplished; goals help to raise our level of achievement.

Take time to set goals with your children. We think you'll find that they enjoy the process and are motivated by achieving their aims. It motivates you, too, as you watch your children develop the maturity, confidence, and independence that come from having specific objectives in life.

Setting goals can lead you to other teaching opportunities with the activities in this book. For example, let's say your child's goal is to save for his own computer. To hit that target, you can use some of the savings and accumulation activities in the Savvy Saver chapter. You can also use Sharp Shopper activities to find the best deal.

Driving and Car Contract

Teaching Goal:
   • To remind your children of the responsibility that accompanies privileges.
Teaching Method:
   • Parents ⇨ Intentional ⇨ As you go
Age Range: 15-18
Sweet Spot Age Range: 16-17

Activity Description:

Perhaps it's something in their genes. Having a car to drive often kicks in as the major goal in life around 14 or 15 years of age. We suggest that driving a car, whether provided by the parents or purchased by industrious children, should have some strings attached.

Before your future cruiser puts the "pedal to the metal," sign a driving contract. This agreement will establish an understanding between you and your child about the requirements, penalties, financial responsibilities, and maintenance duties related to the car.

The following are important considerations to include:

- What maintenance responsibilities will your young driver have? Washing the car, changing the oil, and vacuuming the inside are examples.
- Who pays for gas?
- What portion of the additional insurance cost is paid by your child?
- What grades must be maintained to continue the privilege of driving?
- Who pays for any tickets? Does the answer change if a parent is in the car when the violation occurs?
- Will others be allowed to ride with your child? If so, how many?
- Will you allow talking on the cell phone or listening to music while driving?
- What sanctions or penalties occur if grades are not maintained, expenses are not paid, or maintenance chores are missed?

Background Information:

Cars can become an area of conflict for families. Parents should address the issue of cars and car expenses before it becomes a point of contention with your children. The decisions need to be made in advance and communicated to kids so they have plenty of time to understand and plan for them.

Owning vehicles can be a bottomless pit into which teenagers pour their hard-earned money. Perhaps you remember some hot-rodding, car-crazed people (usually males) from high school who worked to pay for every accessory possible, only to have their grades suffer as they put in long hours on the job just to keep the car or truck going.

I (Jeremy) remember my parents *not* allowing me to buy my own car. As a young, yard-mowing, newspaper-delivering entrepreneur, I saved my money diligently. Knowing that my parents could not afford a car for me on a pastor's salary, I assumed I could buy one with my own money.

My parents vetoed that notion. Though I resented my independence being squelched, I would later (and still) appreciate their preventing me from wasting so much money. They made one of the family cars available for needed transportation. I didn't look so cool driving a van to school, but my parents were very wise. My saved money was used for college, overseas study, and my own debt-free, used car after graduating from college with no student loans!

In our book *The New Master Your Money*, we pointed out that the cheapest car you'll ever own is most likely the car you're presently driving. Contrary to advertising and popular thought, no car is an investment. Only antique cars appreciate in value. Some cars hold their value more than others, but depreciation is the norm, not the exception. A person would be pretty foolish to buy an investment that was guaranteed not to appreciate.

A question we (the Blue family) asked ourselves regarding a car for our children was this: For whose convenience was it? If it was for ours (Ron and Judy's), we would choose the car and pay the expenses.

Living in Atlanta where the traffic and sheer size of the city mean lots of driving time, we felt a car for our teenagers was essential just to reduce our own driving time. So we purchased used—or, as our children would say, ancient—cars for each child at age 16. We were at a point in our business where we could afford to do that.

They used those cars for our convenience, not theirs. If they'd wanted a different car, or if it were for their convenience, the decision would have been different. They would have chosen the car they wanted, but they would have paid for it and all its expenses. Very simply, it was either their choice or ours.

We wanted them to understand two things. First, the real purpose of a car is transportation, not for "show" or style. Second, they needed to know how much it would cost if they chose to drive a car for the sake of appearance, compared to the cost of driving it for transportation purposes.

The issue of cars, and the expenses associated with them, should not be decided solely on the basis of what parents can afford. It should also have something to do with the degree of responsibility shown by the children.

It's amazing how many parents fall into the trap of feeling obliged to give their kids everything those kids desire. The parents forget the purpose of a car. Is it for the convenience of the parents or the children? That really determines who pays.

We required our kids to provide a portion of gas expenses because they used the car sometimes for their own purposes. If they wanted to drive 50 miles on the weekend for entertainment purposes, that was fine as long as they paid for the gas to do so.

How will you and your children remember how you're treating each issue from gas to insurance to breakdowns? Write it down in a driving contract. Refer to it often. Enforce what you decide is prudent in helping your child gain responsibility in this crucial area—even if what you decide is unpopular.

Object Lesson: Money and Bills

Teaching Goals:
- To show your kids where the money comes from and where it goes.
- To teach the importance of planning spending so you have enough for basic needs.

Teaching Method:
- Parents ⇨ Intentional ⇨ Created

Age Range: 4-12

Sweet Spot Age Range: 6-9

Activity Description:

After a payday, bring home $100 in one-dollar bills. Place all the dollar bills on the kitchen table.

Before calling in your kids, gather some objects to represent spending categories. For example, an apple and a box of cereal might represent food; your car keys or a toy car could symbolize transportation costs; a hat or pair of shoes could stand for clothes; an offering envelope and a Bible might represent church offerings.

Include a symbol of your job to represent the income you earn—for example, a hard hat, stethoscope, briefcase, or calculator.

You don't have to represent all the categories of your budget. Use the major ones, such as housing, food, clothing, and giving that your kids are familiar with. Make sure you use at least one or two discretionary categories, such as entertainment, restaurants, or vacation. Also, include the category of taxes. Use a flag or map of your country to represent that.

Explain that you go to work every day in order to earn money. No one gives you money; your parents don't send you money every week. You must go and work for it. Discuss how today was payday and you brought home your money.

Explain that you must pay for things the government provides, like roads, schools, and protection by the military. This is what it costs to live in your country. Put about $25 in the taxes category (adapt this to apply to your nation). Don't bother distinguishing among various kinds of taxes.

Tell your children that a portion of your income is spent on living expenses. Place an amount (using percentages based on your actual spending patterns), say $10, next to the items representing food. Continue placing amounts in each category proportional to the actual costs. Housing, for example, probably should have the most dollars allocated to it.

To remind kids about being a savvy saver, set aside an amount for savings. Rather than going into detail about 401(k) plans or automatic payroll deductions, simply say you're saving some.

After you disperse the dollars, ask your children if they have any questions.

Then add a hypothetical twist. Take back all the money from the categories except taxes and giving. Ask your kids, "What if I was excited after getting paid and spent all my money on _____?" (Fill in the blank with movies, toys, restaurants, or other discretionary items.) Place a large, disproportionate amount next to the object representing that item. Brainstorm what would happen if you misused money in that way.

Background Information:

Kids often think that parents have an endless supply of money. They see you whip out checks, cash, or assorted plastic cards to buy things. Perhaps they witness cash coming out of an ATM when you simply insert a card. Your aim is to show them visually that there is a *limited amount of money,* and you must be careful to have enough for your various needs.

For young children, this may be more currency than they've seen before at one time. This is the effect you want. You work hard for your paycheck; but to buy the things you and your family need, it takes a lot of money.

If both parents work, start with two stacks of dollar bills. Then combine the two piles and explain how you pool both incomes to pay family expenses.

Going Deeper:
Rather than using a proportional activity using $100 in cash, older children can try the following activity of paying actual bills.

Paying the Bills for a Month

Teaching Goals:
  • To show your kids what monthly living expenses are.
  • To provide training in various everyday, adult financial matters.
Teaching Method:
  • Parents ⇨ Intentional ⇨ As you go
Age Range: 12-18
Sweet Spot Age Range: 13-15

Activity Description:
As you pay your bills, walk through the process with your children. Explain the importance of paying people you owe regularly and on time, and recording your transactions.

As you go through this activity, help kids feel like grown-ups. Tell them you have confidence in their ability to help you. You want them to watch you this time, but next time you want them to do it on their own.

Explain your steps. Show them how to complete a check properly.

Have them stuff the envelopes, lick the stamps, and so on. Be watching nearby in the same room. Try to avoid retelling them each step. Let your children ask for help.

Celebrate their successful completion of the activity with pizza or some other treat.

Background Information:
In our family (the Whites), we record our household expenditures with money management software. We've begun to let our older daughter enter transactions. Like most kids, she loves anything to do with the computer.

Here are the aims of this activity:

1. *Preparing your kids to pay bills on their own.* They should know how you track due dates, how you record checks, what receipts or invoices you keep and don't keep, and so on. Most schools don't teach this. Kids need to see your system—whatever that system is.

2. *Letting your teens "know about the flow."* They need to understand how money flows in—and out.

As in many other areas, teens and preteens don't quite understand the full picture of their parents' finances. They may think that if their parents *make* money, their parents must *have* a lot of money. They may think all that money lying around should be used to buy them a car, finance their wardrobes, or pay for all the concerts within driving distance.

You're letting them know what it takes to keep the household going—how much you pay in insurance and taxes, how much the utilities are, etc. You're showing them the great responsibility of providing for all these needs.

Suggest that you may need your kids' help again as a backup. You can benefit by doing some ongoing training with your child in case you and/or your spouse are disabled or unavailable to do bill-paying chores for extended periods of time.

Celebrating Financial Freedom

Teaching Goals:
• To inform your child of her responsibility to make decisions and live with the consequences.

• To describe your future levels of financial support.

Teaching Method:
• Parents ⇨ Intentional ⇨ Created
Age Range: 18-24
Sweet Spot Age Range: 21-23

Activity Description:
When your child has reached an age of maturity, such as after college or after he is engaged, go out for a nice dinner.

Formally bless your child with affirming words. Mention how proud you are of him, how much you love him, and how special he is. Explain how you'll be available to him for support, advice, and prayer, but you'll be making very few decisions for him; he'll be making most of his own.

Describe your level of financial support in the future. Let him know if you'll be helping to pay for advanced degrees or not. You've helped to launch him, but success in life relies on his diligence and wise choices.

Set minimal expectations for future inheritance or large gifts during his lifetime. You might mention whether you're planning to spend much of your estate or donate it.

Share with your child how much confidence you have in him and his future. Remind him that God has plans for a future and a hope (see Jeremiah 29:11).

Background Information:
This activity can be a powerful, momentous event in the life of your child as she moves from childhood to adulthood. In the Blue family, we held a dinner on each child's eighteenth birthday. We do this to celebrate the birthday, but more importantly, to formalize a time of releasing the child. We tell her we've done the best job we could in teaching, counseling, and raising her. Our role in her life will begin to change from that of rule maker to that of friend and counselor.

It may sound almost harsh, but we advised our kids that all

decisions in their lives from that point were theirs. We pledged to help them if they asked us, but we would not make their decisions for them.

As long as they continued to live with us, we asked them to abide by the rules of our household. These rules were very simple and basic, such as sharing in the chores and maintaining their rooms in an orderly manner.

During that celebration dinner we also previewed how we would assist our children financially. We told them what college expenses we would pay for. Anything beyond that was their responsibility. We told them what help to expect regarding automobiles and wedding/honeymoon expenses. We also told them what we would provide and not provide for them financially after marriage.

Every parent must make some of these financial decisions at some point. We simply settled and communicated them in advance. We felt our children needed to know so they could accept the responsibility to plan and manage their lives in accordance with their personal goals, priorities, commitments, and objectives.

Of course, we reminded them that we would always be available for help and counsel on both major and minor decisions. But we made it clear that we would not, to the best of our ability, interfere in their lives. How they raise their children, where they live, and how they manage their money are their decisions.

Initially, our three daughters responded with a bit of fear of being personally accountable. But they adjusted and handled the responsibility extremely well. Our boys seemed to embrace right away the independence available to them. We felt the formal release was vital in helping them feel responsible to make their own decisions.

It's a strange phenomenon with older teenagers and young adults: They want freedom, but may be frightened when it's handed to them. They're not necessarily trying to gain freedom as much as looking to be treated as responsible human beings.

Although my (Jeremy's) daughters are not old enough to begin such conversations, I've known of several wealthy clients who communicated expectations to young adult children. They would say in passing things like, "Our money is set aside for retirement, so we can't help you with buying a house." Or, "If your mother and I don't spend all our net worth, we'll probably designate in our wills that it be given away when we die." They could always change their minds later, yet made it clear they didn't expect to have any thirtysomethings sponging off the "old man's" assets.

Read Books Showing the Wisdom of Prudent Planning

Teaching Goal:
• To persuade your children to be prudent planners.
Teaching Method:
• Their Own Experience ⇨ Others
Age Range: Various

Activity Description:
Even we financial nerds don't enjoy reading boring budgeting books. The following are written in an easy-to-read manner with valuable insights.

Title: *Financial Peace*
Author: Dave Ramsey (Viking, 1997)
Description: This best-selling book propelled Dave Ramsey and his radio show to fame with its practical, hilarious, and humble financial insights. From suggesting we conduct a "plasectomy" on our credit cards to budgeting to investing, Dave provides the "common sense your Grandmother taught"—except he keeps his teeth in.
Length: 66 pages
Age Range: 12-18

Title: *The Purpose-Driven Life*
Author: Rick Warren (Zondervan, 2002)
Description: The most basic questions everyone faces in life, particularly teenagers and young adults: Why am I here? What is my purpose? Most self-help books suggest people should look within, at their own desires and dreams. But Rick Warren says the starting place must be with God and His eternal purposes for each life. This book can help give prudent planners a foundation for their goal setting.
Length: 334 pages
Age Range: 12-18

Title: *How Much Land Does a Man Need?*
Author: Leo Tolstoy (Crocodile Books, 2002)
Description: Pahóm, a simple peasant, believed that with a little more land he could be so content that the devil himself could not unsettle him. But the devil worked Pahóm's desire into his downfall. How much land would be enough? Pahóm soon learned that with more land came a consuming desire for self-protection and a hunger for even more.
Length: 32 pages
Age Range: 8-14

Intelligent Investors

From a Child's Perspective:
When asked why lovers often hold hands:
    "They want to make sure their rings don't fall off because they paid good money for them."—DAVE, AGE 8

"I think kids should get allowances, but they should save them for pets or other important things."—JESSICA, AGE 9

Biblical Principles:
Give portions to seven, yes to eight, for you do not know what disaster may come upon the land.—ECCLESIASTES 11:2

She considers a field and buys it; out of her earnings she plants a vineyard.—PROVERBS 31:16

The Gambling Fool Simulator

Teaching Goal:
   • To illustrate the foolishness of gambling and how unlikely winning the lottery is.

Teaching Method:
  • Parents ⇨ Intentional ⇨ Created
Age Range: 10-18
Sweet Spot Age Range: 12-15

Activity Description:
Announce to your child that you're sponsoring a lottery.

Explain that a portion of the winnings will go to education. Your child could win $1,000 for his college fund and his most desired toy or gadget—a video game system, MP3 player, new bike, etc.

To enter, your child must pay you $1. To win, he must guess the correct number between 1 and 14 million.

(Note: If you're worried about having to pay the jackpot, you probably have an unrealistic faith in the likelihood of winning a lottery. Just in case, don't promise a jackpot you can't afford. Frankly, though, we don't think you'll be making a payout.)

First, write on a slip of paper a number between 1 and 14 million. Don't reveal it. Try to pick a truly random number, not one like your address or zip code, or one rounded to the nearest thousand or ten thousand.

Next, have your child pay you the dollar (no IOUs).

Then ask him to write down any number he chooses between 1 and 14 million.

Finally, let your child compare the number you chose and the one he chose. You can be practically certain they won't match.

Explain that your child lost the $1 in the hope of getting $1,000.

Point out briefly the dangers of gambling, using your own knowledge and the "Background Information" in this activity.

Ask if he wants to play again. If not, try to coax him to do so by saying you'll give him six picks for another dollar.

When he eventually gives up, congratulate him on the wisdom of stopping. Explain that you were only pretending to encourage him.

Discuss the advertising approaches of the lotteries. Mention that just because lotteries say the money will be used for education doesn't mean it's a smart idea to participate. Lotteries and other "games of chance" take much-needed funds from many families, giving just enough to "good" causes to make gambling socially acceptable.

Background Information:
Lotteries and other forms of gambling, legal in so many places and under consideration in others, may seem like a recent phenomenon. But even the Bible talks about "casting lots," an ancient form of gambling.

Your kids probably have seen lottery billboards, heard references to "winning the jackpot," or observed transactions involving scratch-off game tickets at the gas station. How sad and strange that governments promote the idea of beating the odds and having it all.

Duke University professors have pointed out that "the states now offering lotteries do not simply make a product available in order to accommodate the widespread taste for buying a low-priced chance at a big prize. They seek to foster that taste."[1]

One of the commissioners on the National Gambling Impact Study Commission (NGISC)—charged by the U.S. Congress to conduct a study on the impact of gambling—mentioned in a recent speech, "Lotteries have propagated the myth that gambling is good for society in general and the government in particular. Lotteries are perhaps the hardest form of gambling to justify in terms of their costs and benefits. The best studies all point in the same direction: Lotteries prey on the poor and the undereducated."[2]

Your kids are up against a powerful marketing force. The NGISC report cited the example of Ohio's Super Lotto game; its advertising plan stated that ads and promotions should be timed to coincide with the receipt of Social Security and disability checks. Explain to your kids that many adults are "tricked" into buying lottery tickets. They don't get richer, only poorer.

Understanding the hugely unfavorable odds is a rather abstract concept. Losing a few dollars is much less abstract. We chose the

number 14 million because one in 14 million is the chance of winning the California Lotto Jackpot.[3] The odds for the multi-state
Powerball lottery are one in 146 million![4]

Gambling is not God's desire. Willing work, savvy saving, intelligent investing—those are the paths to wealth. Despite our collo-
quial comments about "my lucky stars," some mystic "destiny" or
"fate," superstitious symbols of clover or rabbit's feet, or "Lady Luck
smiling," God is sovereign and controls all outcomes. *The lot is cast
into the lap, but its every decision is from the LORD"* (Proverbs 16:33).

God's principle is never "Get rich quick," but rather, "Work
hard, give hard, save hard. Be fully content." Gambling contradicts
these biblical values at the expense of many precious, needy families.

Going Deeper:

If your child quickly understands that betting is a bad deal, this
activity has been a success. If he wants to keep playing and losing his
own money, let him do so a few times. But explain each time that
you're certain he won't win. Don't let him lose too many times. Even
some adults don't "get it" and lose until their resources are gone.

If your child doesn't want to play at all, coax him. Use the same
appeals that lotteries do ("You might be the winner!" or "Think
how much fun you could have with that toy!").

After you've used this activity with your children, point out
billboards, TV commercials, and radio ads promoting gambling.
Ask your child to pick out the deceptive claims and emotional persuasion methods used.

Candy Day

Teaching Goals:
- To establish early patterns of delayed gratification, which are
  important for investing.
- To prevent "spoiling" of kids and to establish boundaries.

Teaching Method:
  • Parents ⇨ Intentional ⇨ As You Go
Age Range: 2-10
Sweet Spot Age Range: 4-7

Activity Description:
Most parents of younger children brace themselves for the dreaded trek through the checkout aisle of the store. When your child sees the rows of candy, you know the question is coming.

On the really tough days, you're afraid of the tantrum. You don't want to start (or restart) a pattern of giving in and building expectations every time you pass that candy rack. But you fear the social workers may come when your child wails at being told no.

Delayed gratification is the key trait of financial maturity. To have any surplus to invest someday, a person must delay spending and exhibit self-control.

Toward that end, here's a simple activity to try in your family.

Establish one day a week as Candy Day. On that day, kids can eat as much candy as they like (within reason, within your budget, and within dietary restrictions). Saturday may be the best day to manage any "sugar highs." But this is the *only* day they eat candy.

If your children receive candy as a gift from grandparents or as a prize at school or church, they must save it until Candy Day. If you do buy candy at the checkout aisle, they must wait until Candy Day to eat it.

Families who've tried this activity report that their children usually tire of eating candy on Candy Day before they've finished it all. Because you know your kids best, you may wish to make Candy Day a temporary experiment—say for one month. Or keep it for a longer period to build their delayed-gratification muscles.

Background Information:
Implicit in the term "delayed gratification" is some eventual gratification. Otherwise, it's punishment.

If you start with this simple activity and later advance to more creative ones, your children can begin a discipline of delayed gratification that will help them financially and in other areas of life.

Why don't more people invest? Because they're not very good at delayed gratification. Investing is simply not consuming all you have today. You set some aside now in the hope it will turn into much more later.

Delayed gratification is also the underlying basis of talking to kids about waiting until marriage for sex. You're not saying no forever; you're just urging them to have the best of what God has in mind for them—later.

Corn Kernels and the Power of Investing

Teaching Goals:
  • To illustrate the multiplying effect of an investment.
  • To show the risks in investing.
Teaching Method:
  • Parents ➪ Intentional ➪ As You Go
Age Range: 4-14
Sweet Spot Age Range: 8-12

Activity Description:
During mid-to-late summer when gardens are producing, obtain a full ear of fresh corn.

Have your child count the number of kernels. This may be a good opportunity to use multiplication. Count the number of kernels in a row. Then count the number of rows encircling the cob and multiply. (Hint: Most ears of corn have approximately 600-660 kernels.)

If possible, take your kids to a garden or a cornfield. Ask how many ears of corn are on each stalk of corn. (Most stalks of corn produce two ears.)

Have your children total the number of kernels produced by one stalk of corn. Assume the other ear would have the same number of kernels as your sample. Kids can either add up the two numbers or multiply by two.

Ask: How many kernels of corn did the farmer plant to make over 1,200 kernels?

Answer: one. Talk about how one kernel planted could later result in so much.

Then ask your kids about possible risks in this "investment." What are some bad things that could have happened to the corn while it was growing? Depending on your children's experience with gardening and planting, you may have to give them some hints: not enough rain; animals (deer, raccoons, wild turkey) eating the corn; pests such as bugs and worms damaging the leaves or ears; storms blowing down the stalks.

Ask: What would happen if the farmer ate every bit of the corn this year and didn't save any seeds to plant next year?

Background Information:
Explain how this word picture applies to your family.

Your "harvest" initially is the paycheck you bring home. You've sown effort, energy, skills, and time. Your harvest is the money you earn. It's important to save some of that money to "plant" for other crops. You don't want to "eat your seed corn."

Observe that by investing, you hope to yield more of a harvest. This is particularly important if something happens to your "harvest" at your job.

Going Deeper:
With older children, you can have a more in-depth discussion about reaping and harvesting after reading Galatians 6:7: *"Do not be deceived: God cannot be mocked. A man reaps what he sows."*

Ask kids the following: In this simple statement, "You reap what you sow," what truths do you find about both investing and life?

Discuss with older children the following four laws of the harvest. Discuss the application these laws have to investing, then look for deeper meanings connected to life and spiritual matters.

1. *You reap more than you sow.* A multiplying effect is possible.

2. *You reap after you sow.* Patience and time are necessary. Nothing happens immediately; results are longer-term.

3. *You reap the character and nature of what you sow.* You plant corn, you get corn, not tomatoes.

4. *You reap only if you sow.* Some effort and risk must be expended. Nothing comes automatically. It's a conditional promise: *If* you sow, you will reap.

The Rule of 72

Teaching Goal:
- To provide a quick formula describing how long it takes an investment to double with compounding.

Teaching Method:
- Parents ➪ Intentional ➪ As You Go

Age Range: 10-18

Sweet Spot Age Range: 12-16

Activity Description:

As you're driving down the road, ask your child this question: "How long would it take $100 to double if it earned 8 percent interest per year and the interest was added back to the investment each year?"

After getting a dazed look from your child, tell him you can do the math without even using a calculator, computer, or pencil. You'll use the Rule of 72.

Explain that the Rule of 72 is a formula that quickly tells you approximately how many years it takes for your money to double. Simply take the number 72 divided by the interest rate. The result is the number of years for the investment to double.

This ingenious shortcut even takes compounding into effect. In this example, 72 divided by 8 percent results in nine years. When you're back home, ask your child to take out a piece of paper and label columns as follows. Ask him to complete the chart for several different interest rates similar to the example:

72 Divided by Interest Rate = Years to Double Investment

	Interest Rate	Years to Double
Example	12%	6

Review the results. Ask whether the interest rate makes a big difference. Then ask, "How much longer would a person have to wait for his money to double if he settled for a 3 percent rate compared to a 9 percent rate?"

Background Information:
The actual mathematical formulas used to compute the future value of an amount of money are complicated—even for financial nerds like us. This formula isn't precise to the penny, but it's reasonably close.

The key application point is that a small difference in the rate of return can make a big difference in the total return. A person can obtain a higher rate of return, on average, by taking on more risk. Investing in a business, for example, can offer a potentially higher return than putting money in a savings account.

Play Monopoly

Teaching Goal:
  • To learn truths about investing, real estate returns, and risk using a "hands-on" approach.
Teaching Method:
  • Parents ⇨ Intentional ⇨ As You Go
Age Range: 8-18
Sweet Spot Age Range: 9-13

Activity Description:

Financial games provide the marvelous benefits of playing and learning as a family. Chess and backgammon have been used throughout history to teach military strategy or leadership. You can learn financial lessons with a classic game found in many homes: Monopoly.

Purchase or dig out of the closet the classic version of Monopoly. Though you can find almost every variation under the sun—Muppets Monopoly, Star Wars Monopoly, and even Disney Princess Monopoly Junior—we think the classic version is best for teaching the basic lessons.

Take time to learn the rules and teach them to your children. Play the game more than once. Repetition improves learning and builds confidence.

Discuss strategies at the end of each game. What worked well? What caused financial problems? In as simple a way as possible, talk about how you've seen some of these successful and unsuccessful strategies played out in real life.

Point out key financial truths as you play. Use a fun, eager-to-play tone, not your correcting or lecturing voice. On the following page are a few truths to get you started.

Have fun, spend time together, and interject some of your own observations of how Monopoly reflects real-world finances.

Background Information:

While today's electronic games easily capture our attention, board games provide the benefit of interacting with real, live people. Playing games involves giving, taking, talking, discussing, moving, watching, counting, and so on. Many children learn better through the "hands-on" experience of a game than by listening to lectures or reading books.

Playing Monopoly provides practice in counting money, making change, and organizing funds. As you work through the game,

Real Life	Monopoly
Paychecks provide regular liquidity to help you survive.	The $200 as you pass "Go" is like a regular paycheck helping you pay bills and restore reserves.
Paychecks alone are not enough to build wealth.	It's hard to win by only going around the board. You must invest and buy some properties.
Investing requires some risk.	You can buy a property hoping that another player will land on it, but there's no guarantee. You may never recoup your money.
Investing may provide outstanding returns and build substantial wealth.	You may receive far more than you ever paid for the property. You probably have a better chance of winning if you buy more properties.
You must manage your cash flow wisely.	Buying too many properties too quickly may result in bankruptcy.
Start small and grow your wealth gradually. Get-rich-quick schemes rarely work.	You gradually buy properties. You save to buy a house, then another, then another. You can't win Monopoly in 10 minutes.
Some elements of success or failure are beyond your control.	The Chance cards or the roll of the dice can affect the outcome of the game.
The more expensive real estate may yield more rental income.	Park Place and Boardwalk cost more than Baltic Avenue or Connecticut Avenue, but they yield much more rental income.

talk about what a mortgage means. Explain what a deed is. Show your children the deed to your house or your mortgage document. Games also provide you with insight into your kids' behavioral tendencies. If your children tend to take big risks, they may do so in games. If they're indecisive, you'll see indicators. If they're prone to bend the rules or cheat, you may catch glimpses of that. If they're risk averse, you'll see them playing cautiously.

Going Deeper:

- Consider introducing your children to a real-life example of people who've built some wealth or real estate holdings the "Monopoly way." You may have a friend or family member (or be one yourself) who started with a house or two, gradually added more, and now owns several properties. If you approach such a person with respect and a willingness to learn from her wisdom (rather than just being nosy), she likely will share how she started, what she learned, and how she did it.
- Balance the Monopoly training with deeper insight about relationships. The object of Monopoly is to bankrupt the other players and financially crush them. In real life, however, we should help each other succeed. Teamwork is vital. Helping others do well will help you do well.
- Look for broader stewardship truths. Discuss with your child how all the money and deeds go back in the box at the end of the game. Similarly, God owns everything in this life. We're able to manage and use it for a while, but we leave the world with nothing—just as we walk away from a Monopoly game empty-handed.

⁓⁓⁓⁓⁓

Play Cashflow for Kids

Teaching Goals:
- To teach children how to manage their personal cash flow.

• To teach more complex financial terms and concepts.
Teaching Method:
• Parents ⇨ Intentional ⇨ As You Go
Age Range: 6-14
Sweet Spot Age Range: 8-12

Activity Description:
Created by Robert Kiyosaki, author of *Rich Dad, Poor Dad,* the game Cashflow for Kids is designed specifically for teaching financial literacy. It's also entertaining, colorful, and engaging. Available at www.richdad.com, this game breaks down more difficult concepts, such as the advantages of passive income, for both you and your child.

Because it was designed to teach, Cashflow for Kids is a better game than Monopoly in these respects:
• It emphasizes sources of passive income besides real estate. It also provides for investments in mutual funds and stocks. Participants can start a business to supplement their income.
• The winner does not have to drive the others to the shame of bankruptcy.
• It incorporates the level of one's lifestyle and expenses. The higher the level of lifestyle, the more income must be generated to win.

Background Information:
How many times were you asked as a child, "What do you want to be when you grow up?"

Society and the educational system often focus on what a person will do to earn money. Just as important, however, is making plans to keep and grow the money a person earns. The sooner you can encourage your kids to invest, the more likely they'll do so.

This game introduces and emphasizes an idea that many adults never seem to grasp. With other sources of income working for you (investments, real estate investments, businesses), you can have more options and financial freedom.

Investment Activity to Track Stocks

Teaching Goal:
- To practice investing in the stock market, and to learn the potential returns and risks.

Teaching Method:
- Parents ⇨ Intentional ⇨ Created

Age Range: 9-16
Sweet Spot Age Range: 11-14

Activity Description:
Raid your Monopoly game and take enough $500 bills to distribute $5,000 for each child.

Lead your children in brainstorming about some of the trends and companies they think will be successful in the future. Kids commonly will list consumer brands they're familiar with—their favorite fast-food restaurant, favorite toy, or favorite designer line of clothing. These are good choices for this activity.

Tell them you're going to have an investment contest allowing them to choose three companies in which to buy stock. (Note: The companies must be publicly traded, with stock available to the public. A privately owned local pizza restaurant may not have its company shares available through a stock exchange.)

Obtain the business or financial section of your local newspaper, or a business newspaper such as *The Wall Street Journal*. Look in the stock market tables and find the column for "Price," meaning the price per share of stock. It may be expressed as 59³/₄. This means that each share is valued at $59.75. Your child will likely not have enough money to "buy" many shares. Ask him how he'd like to divide his $5,000 among the three companies he chose.

On a computer spreadsheet (or using lined paper), list the following headings:

<u>Date</u> <u>Company</u> <u>Price/Share</u> <u>Shares Purchased</u> <u>Total Invested</u>

Set the time limit for the period to be tracked. Though investing is best thought of as long-term, you may want to accelerate the learning period and limit the activity to two or three months.

Update the spreadsheet at the end of each week. Have your children look up the price in the paper and compute the new value of their portfolio. Keep a record so you can review with your children the ups and downs their portfolios experience.

Celebrate at the end of the activity. Congratulate your children on investing their money and owning a very, very small part of businesses in your economy.

Background Information:
Taking a risk and owning businesses are important parts of capitalist economies. You may not feel qualified to lead an activity in this area, but children need to be aware of the basic concepts.

Even if your children don't grow up to own stock outright, their retirement plans probably will be invested in the stock market. They may have a 401(k), 403(b), IRA, or pension invested there.

Going Deeper:
- For the sake of simplicity, you may wish to ignore the effects of dividends in this activity. Dividends do play a very important role in the total return of an investment. If your knowledge and your children's ages allow, feel free to factor these in.
- Your older children may wish to do more research for their stock selections. They can go to a company's Web site and request an annual report. On the Internet, they can see the recent stock performance and what other analysts (such as http://finance.yahoo.com) think about the company.

- After going through this exercise of owning specific company stocks, you may wish to try a trial run in mutual funds. Mutual funds provide diversification by enabling investors to own stock in many companies. If you have a financial advisor, he or she can provide you with more information about mutual fund opportunities.

〰〰〰〰

Buy One Share of Stock

Teaching Goal:
- To provide a tangible experience of owning stock in a company.

Teaching Method:
- Parents ➩ Intentional ➩ Created

Age Range: 8-14
Sweet Spot Age Range: 9-12

Activity Description:

Obtaining a small number of shares through a traditional broker isn't practical. Transaction fees at a typical brokerage firm can cost a high percentage of the total purchase. The usual trade on Wall Street is a "round lot" of at least 100 shares.

Consider obtaining one share of stock through a Web-based company specializing in small purchases for children. An example is OneShare.com. This site provides an actual share of stock in its certificate form. You can get a Coke, McDonald's, or Disney stock certificate framed and personalized.

This purchase should be seen mainly as a gift and teaching tool rather than an investment. The framing, transfer fee, and shipping will likely cost more than the share itself. Through the My First Stock Program, your child receives a share of stock, an investment book, and a framed certificate with colorful lettering.

Background Information:
Owning even a sliver of an actual company can make your children more attuned to business and economic matters. The idea is to expose them in a fun, gentle way to an important part of economic life.

Just think what might have happened if your parents had bought you some General Electric or Disney stock 30 or 40 years ago! Obtain stock of a company that your child is familiar with—such as a cereal company, clothing store, restaurant, or toy maker.

Read Books for Intelligent Investing

Teaching Goal:
  • To show your children the rewards of setting aside money so that its value can grow.
Teaching Method:
  • Their Own Experience ⇨ Others
Age Range: Various

Activity Description:
We all need a little motivation to have the discipline to save in order to enjoy future rewards. We think your children will be inspired by reading the examples of success found in these books.

Title: *Rich Dad, Poor Dad: What the Rich Teach their Kids about Money that the Poor and Middle Class Don't*
Author: Robert Kiyosaki (Warner Books, 2000)
Description: A true story about the author's father and his best friend's father. One was rich, the other wasn't. One was educated and the other never finished high school. Both men were strong, dynamic, successful, honest, and hardworking—but they had different ideas when it came to money. This book challenges

conventional (and often wrong) beliefs about how financial success is achieved.

Length: 207 pages
Age Range: 12-18

Title: *Beating the Street*
Author: Peter Lynch (Simon & Schuster, 1993)
Description: Written by the folksy, successful manager at Fidelity Magellan Fund (until 1990), this book provides the basics of finding and researching good ideas to invest in (look in your local town for successful companies). His examples are readable and interesting. The 21 "Peter's principles" range from the simple ("Being first in line is a great idea except on the edge of a cliff") to the in-depth.

Length: 336 pages
Age Range: 14-18

Willing Workers

From a Child's Perspective:
"What does your father do?" Bill Cosby asked one five-year-old
   boy.
"He's a fund-raiser," the boy replied.
"For whom does he raise funds?"
"Himself."[1]

Even if you get an allowance, still think about working for
money. It gets you more money and builds more muscle.
—ANDREW, AGE 10

Biblical Principles:
Lazy hands make a man poor, but diligent hands bring wealth.
—PROVERBS 10:4

*Whatever you do, work at it with all your heart, as working for the
Lord, not for men.*—COLOSSIANS 3:23

*A little sleep, a little slumber, a little folding of the hands to rest—and
poverty will come on you like a bandit and scarcity like an armed
man.*—PROVERBS 24:33-34

Hire Your Children at Home

Teaching Goals:
 • To provide additional opportunities to earn money.
 • To recognize the effort it takes to earn money.
Teaching Method:
 • Parents ⇨ Intentional ⇨ Created
Age Range: 6-18
Sweet Spot Age Range: 8-14

Activity Description:

Post a list of chores your kids can do for extra money. Call it your "For Hire" list. Put it on the refrigerator or family bulletin board.

Beside each job, include the amount to be paid for the work and how frequently it can be done. Here are some examples:
 • Pull weeds from landscaped areas (once a month in summer)
 • Scrub the bottom of the shower, tub, or tiled area (once a week)
 • Clean out the garage (twice a year)
 • Wash windows (three times a year)
 • Vacuum the cars (as needed)
 • Wash the cars (as needed)
 • Dust or wipe baseboards throughout the house (three times a year)
 • Rake leaves (once a year in fall)

Inspect your child's work after it's finished. Your aim isn't to nitpick, but to let your child know that paid labor is evaluated. Throughout life her work will be reviewed, verified, signed off on, approved or disapproved. Reduce the pay if the quality of work doesn't meet your expectations. State this clearly verbally and in writing at the bottom of the job list so your child realizes haphazard work doesn't cut it!

The ideal "chores for hire" are the occasional ones requiring extra effort, not the routine ones of clearing the table or making a bed.

Background Information:
In both of our homes, we've made certain jobs optional—beyond daily, required chores. Our children receive compensation for these jobs. In this way, they learn extra money is available when they're willing to trade their labor and time.

Earning money strictly for savings doesn't come naturally to most kids. They almost always work to earn money for something they need or want *now*. This motivation is okay, however, because we're attempting to teach them that time and effort can be traded for money and other rewards. The long-term perspective will come with more maturity and with the activities provided in Chapter 8.

Educate your kids. Teach them to work, save up, and then buy. Don't let your kids simply nag you for money. Nagging and whining are not effective life skills. Try nagging in your workplace. You'll be cleaning out your desk!

Going Deeper:
Don't require your kids to work and work without ever allowing them to spend some of their money on their choices. It may seem like misspending to you. But it's better for them to learn to tell themselves, "I didn't really need that!" by misspending on $10 and $15 items than to have you control all their spending until adulthood.

When kids who've had no freedom to spend suddenly find themselves with a paycheck and seemingly unlimited options, unfortunate things can happen. They have no idea what things really cost—and no bad personal experiences to warn them to think and wait.

Hire Your Children at Your Business

Teaching Goals:
- To provide practical work experience.
- To provide a tax-efficient way of paying allowances.

Teaching Method:
- Parents ⇨ Intentional ⇨ Created

Age Range: 8-18
Sweet Spot Age Range: 11-16

Activity Description:

If you own a business, paying wages to your child can be a tax-efficient way of shifting income. If the child is under 18, there's no tax for the employer to pay. Plus, the child can earn up to approximately $5,000 without owing income tax. The parent receives a tax deduction for the business and pays no employer payroll tax, and the child receives tax-free income. For details, talk with your tax advisor.

To implement this in your business, the child must provide real service. This may include filing, cleaning an office, helping with mail-outs, vacuuming, taking out the trash, acting as a laborer, or performing other services. The child must render the services and the payments must be made promptly. The payments must be reasonable in relation to the services provided by the child.

As in the "Hire Your Children at Home" activity, we recommend that you post a list of chores that are available and how much you'll pay. For tax purposes, keep a record of the work done.

Paying your children for actual labor in the workplace builds practical experience. It provides them a familiar, safe work environment instead of late-night shifts at a convenience store or fast food restaurant.

Background Information:

If you don't have a business, see the "Hire Your Children at Home" activity. Or find a trustworthy friend or relative for whom your children can work. Accompany them if necessary; never leave them in an uncomfortable situation.

Think creatively. You may very well come up with a great opportunity for your child to gain skills, confidence, and income!

Going Deeper:
You can further enhance the tax benefits of hiring your children at your business by contributing to a Roth IRA for them. This is a tax-free way to save for retirement. Your child's retirement is a long way off, but the potential to build an investment through the power of compounding is staggering.

The only requirement for your child to start a Roth IRA is that he has earned income. You don't have to contribute the money earned by the child. In other words, if the child earns $2,000 and keeps it all, you can contribute $2,000 to a Roth IRA on his behalf. Consult a tax advisor for details on the current maximum yearly contribution.

Job Contract

Teaching Goal:
- To define and agree on the boundaries for your child's work outside the home.

Teaching Method:
- Parents ⇨ Intentional ⇨ Created

Age Range: 12-18
Sweet Spot Age Range: 14-18

Activity Description:
Most parents hope their kids will get off the couch and get some work experience while still in the nest. Unfortunately, some parents have found that the hoped-for job can bring unintended consequences: drop-off in grades at school, missing important

family events, unavailable for church involvement, and so on.

When your young person is searching for a job, let him or her know about your rules and the veto power you retain. For example, working the night shift as a security guard may not fit your safety requirements; wearing skimpy, skin-tight hostess attire may not fit your modesty standards.

After your child finds a job of interest, write a contract. This serves as an understanding between you and your child about your expectations.

It's not a legal, binding contract enforceable in a court of law. But it should specify responsibilities and limits. For example, you may want to include items such as the following:

- Maximum number of hours. What are the time limits during the school year and during the summer?
- Minimum grades to maintain at school.
- The child's responsibility for getting to work on time and dressing properly. Avoid being the one to wake your child every working day. Help her learn the lesson, "If you want your dreams to come true, don't oversleep." Perhaps a boss addressing the problem or firing her will be a better way to teach responsibility than nagging her yourself.
- How will he get to and from work? If he uses the family car to deliver pizzas, what is he expected to pay for?
- How will conflicts in scheduling be resolved? You may require no working on holidays, for example. You may still want your teenager to go on the scheduled family vacation.
- Physical safety requirements.
- Guidelines for use of earnings (tithing and savings percentages, for example).

Background Information:

Reaching an understanding with your child in advance helps to reduce conflict and helps both of you think through potential problems. Write the contract and sign it. As the old saying goes, "The shortest pencil is better than the longest memory."

~~~~~~~~~~~~~

Become a Business Incubator

Teaching Goals:
- To encourage your children to start a business and meet needs.
- To teach the basic operations of a business.

Teaching Method:
- Parents ⇨ Intentional ⇨ Created
- Children ⇨ Their Own Money ⇨ Created

Age Range: 9-18
Sweet Spot Age Range: 12-16

Activity Description:
As you observe your children's talents, interests, and gifts, watch for business opportunities for them as well. You can help them hatch a new venture. Move beyond the traditional one-time lemonade stands and branch into areas where your children could actually earn money.

Brainstorm ideas. Traditional self-employment opportunities are still good ones: lawn mowing, babysitting, newspaper delivery. Others may be possible, such as the following:
- Web site design
- Pet sitting
- Dog walking services
- Pet grooming
- Being a clown for birthday parties and other events
- Tutoring others in academic subjects
- Teaching a skill—tennis, computer skills, or a musical instrument

Make a business plan. It doesn't have to be an inch-thick document full of graphs, but sketch out the opportunities. What are the risks involved? Is there competition? How will you advertise? Are there safety factors?

Encourage your child to set up and develop good administrative habits: keeping receipts, filing, sending bills, returning calls promptly.

Consider whether you should be involved by providing counsel, start-up funds, loans, or transportation. How can you help the business succeed without doing all the work for your child?

Background Information:

The term "business incubator" refers to organizations that help emerging growth companies survive the start-up period when they're most vulnerable. (There's even a National Business Incubation Association that "advances the business creation process to increase entrepreneurial success and individual opportunity," according to its Web site.[2])

As a parent, you can serve as a business incubator primarily by giving encouragement and making your child aware of opportunities. When one of the White daughters started a craft business, we used our influence to introduce our friends to her products. Many of her first customers were friends. After selling a few items, she began to become more interested and branched out to craft shows.

A client has a son who started a lawn mowing business when he was 12 years old. The dad financed the startup. The son paid the loans back, and by the time he graduated from high school, had saved $10,000 and had purchased almost $30,000 worth of equipment. He was able to sell his business and the equipment and fund his way through college. That young man learned financial responsibility!

Profits and Payback

Teaching Goal:
- To teach the true costs of having a business.

Teaching Method:
- Parents ⇨ Intentional ⇨ Created
- Children ⇨ Their Own Money ⇨ Created

Age Range: 10-18
Sweet Spot Age Range: 14-18

Activity Description:
As we discussed in the "Become a Business Incubator" activity, your children can learn some excellent lessons from developing a small business and providing services for others. If your kids have set up an ongoing small business, you may have a good opportunity to implement a reimbursement plan.

To help your children understand the costs involved in owning a business, you may need to charge them for what you provide. We're not necessarily suggesting that your six-year-old daughter setting up a lemonade stand pay you for every ice cube. But pre-teens and teenagers need to understand all the costs of their service or products. Knowing the full cost helps them in pricing, making decisions about expanding, or evaluating how much they earn compared to other jobs.

Here are some guidelines in setting up the reimbursement:
- After the business has grown, let your children know that they need to start reimbursing you for their business expenses.
- Help your children practice negotiation skills. Ask them what they think is a fair amount.
- Separate purchases at the store if they're used entirely and directly for your children; show the receipt to them and ask to be repaid.
- Try to recover some, but not all, costs. You're not looking to make profit off your children—just to get some reimbursement.

- Charge for the larger items (use of lawn mower or computer, significant postage, etc.).
- Avoid charging for minor items (electricity, small supplies you already have on hand, etc.).

Background Information:

One client's son wanted to use his dad's mower to start a business. The dad agreed and served as a helpful incubator to get the business birthed. After the first summer, the father decided to charge his son for using his mower and tools.

My (Jeremy's) daughter learned to make handmade greeting cards. She began making them for others and selling them. We encouraged her and promoted them to friends. She made attractive sample cards to show others. Occasionally she would sell a card, then make a replacement card from the craft supplies we already had available.

A family friend invited her to share a booth at a local arts and crafts festival. To build up her inventory, she had to make dozens of cards. Because she'd used up much of our family craft supplies, we told her she'd have to pay for the new ones. She needed to understand she was taking a risk—paying for supplies before inventory was sold. She also needed to know what her costs were to determine reasonable prices. Reluctantly she agreed—already seeing her margins being cut.

Fortunately, she sold most of her cards at the festival. She was able to pay for supplies and enjoy profit.

We felt strongly, however, that allowing her to keep all the proceeds while having us pay for all the supplies was unfair to us as parents and to her as a budding entrepreneur. Parents are tempted to unduly reward the initiative and self-discipline their kids exhibit, but sometimes generous rewards cost kids the dose of reality they need to succeed.

Read Willing Worker Books

Teaching Goal:
- To build a good work ethic by reinforcing the value and benefits of labor.

Teaching Method:
- Their Own Experience ➪ Others

Age Range: Various

Activity Description:
Kids best learn by doing. But you need all the resources you can find to convince them of the value of work. A little motivation from books like these will help get them started.

Title: *A Job for Jenny Archer*
Author: Ellen Conford (Little, Brown, 1990)
Description: Jenny wants to buy her Mom a fur coat. She tries many ways to earn money. Instead of a coat, Jenny finds the perfect gift in a most unlikely place.
Length: 80 pages
Age Range: 6-7

Title: *The Toothpaste Millionaire*
Author: Jean Merrill (Houghton Mifflin, 1999)
Description: Rufus makes his own toothpaste. He starts selling it and earns money. His friends help him turn his business into something great.
Length: 96 pages
Age Range: 10-13

Title: *Go Getter: A Story That Tells You How to Be One*
Author: Peter Kyne (Henry Holt & Co., 2005)
Description: An interesting parable forms this 1921 classic, read by generations of businesspeople. Its main topics are focus and determination. A "never-say-die" salesman is given a challenge and

gets it done. The tale moves quickly with vivid characters and well-timed suspense. The real lesson is the timeless one of how to identify what's important on a job and succeed through a flat-out desire to finish it. Recommended for "extra credit" reading.

Length: 96 pages
Age Range: 14-18

PART III

Frequently
Asked
Questions

Here's My Challenge: Questions from Real, Live Parents

From a Child's Perspective:

To a boy of six named Paul, Bill Cosby once asked, "What does your father do?"

"He's a banker," Paul replied. "He banked into a parked car one time."

"Was he trying to collect on a loan?"

"No, he's not alone. He's in a whole bank full of bankers."

"Does he do anything special in the bank?"

"He does money there."

"You mean he prints it?"

"I think so. I'll ask him."[1]

A little girl became restless as the preacher's sermon dragged on and on. Finally, she leaned over to her mother and whispered, "Mommy, if we give him the money now, will he let us go?"

Biblical Principles:

Fathers, do not exasperate your children; instead, bring them up in the training and instruction of the Lord.—EPHESIANS 6:4

Discipline your son, for in that there is hope.—PROVERBS 19:18

Through the years we've counseled many parents struggling with their kids over money management. Perhaps some of these challenges also occur in your family. Here are some specific problems, our recommended solutions, and some guiding principles.

Challenge: One Child Taking Financial Advantage of a Sibling

What do you do with a child who sells toys or clothing to a younger sibling at an exorbitant price? Or, what about the child who has the ability to con his sibling out of what he wants at far too cheap a price? Or, how do you handle the one who borrows from his siblings and never repays them?

Potential Solutions

In our experience, every family with more than one child has to face this challenge at some time.

Just as courts settle business and financial disputes, parents should always reserve the right to be judges or arbitrators in these situations. Your word is the final word. We believe that after the first time, you should impose a penalty for further unfair transactions.

In most instances, the penalty should be a monetary one. Let's say your older child buys his brother's new baseball, which cost four dollars, for 25 cents. Consider requiring that the purchaser pay the full fair value of four dollars plus a two-dollar penalty. Make sure the penalty applies even if the perpetrator decides to give back the baseball.

Principles

It's important to deal with this behavior so the unjust winner doesn't develop an attitude problem. The book of Proverbs says that the Lord hates a false balance. Some have paraphrased this to say that "cheaters never win and winners never cheat."

In other words, be fair with one another. The issue needs to be dealt with firmly to avoid bitterness between siblings and to correct the wrong behavior.

God loves the sinner but hates the sin. Don't let the sinful action—or its root causes of greed and deceit—continue.

Challenge: How Much to Give as an Allowance

How much should I give my children as allowances? What chores should I require my children to perform?

Potential Solutions

We think an allowance should be a teaching tool to help children learn about money. You're there to guide and direct, but kids learn from handling their own finances.

An allowance isn't welfare, but a benefit for being a member of the family. Just as there are benefits like allowances, there are responsibilities like regular chores.

One rule of thumb used by some financial counselors through the years is an allowance of $1 per week multiplied by your child's age. Thus, an 8-year old gets $8 per week. That may sound high. But with this approach, your child should be paying some of his own expenses (school lunches, clothes, etc.).

For reference, here are the results of a survey published in *The Wall Street Journal*.[2]

Age Group	Percentage Receiving Allowance	Average Weekly Amount*
15-17	57	$19.30
12-14	67	$11.30
9-11	56	$8.00
6-8	50	$6.00

* Of those receiving an allowance.

We're not suggesting this be your child's allowance. That's your decision. We simply thought this information would satisfy your curiosity about what others do.

In Chapter 4 of this book we suggest setting an allowance (or the funding of specific categories) to cover your child's needs. That's probably a better way to determine an allowance instead of some arbitrary amount times an age.

We've required our children to complete certain chores just because they're members of our family. They must assume part of the responsibility for living in our household. These chores include keeping a clean room, setting the table, loading the dishwasher, and helping with the laundry. They've received no payment for doing these chores. Responsibility for the tasks began at a very early age, and increased in scope as the children got older.

Principles

Our children receive allowances to teach them about money by having their own experience with it. In other words, we don't tie the payment of an allowance to the completion of chores. The two aren't dependent on each other. If you paid for every chore, what would you do when the child refused because he had enough money or wasn't motivated by money?

In addition to required chores, certain jobs around the house are optional. Our kids receive compensation for these tasks. (See the "Hire Your Children at Home" activity in Chapter 11.) It helps them learn they can earn extra money if they trade time for it—and, in turn, must trade their money for things they want to buy.

Challenge: Forgetting to Give an Allowance

Not long ago we asked a 14-year-old girl how her parents handled her allowance. She told us that she no longer received an allowance because her parents could never seem to remember to give it to her. She constantly had to ask for the allowance, so her parents, in frustration, decided to give her money "as she needs it."

Potential Solutions

You might pick a specific day of the month to give the allowance and never vary from that—perhaps the day you pay your bills, or a payday. You'll be less likely to forget one of these regularly occurring events or dates.

This situation seems to be common. Parents can't seem to remember to give an allowance consistently. So they throw up their hands in defeat and revert to giving money as children ask for it.

Another approach that we've found to be very workable is to give the allowance (or fund the categories) on the first day of the month. I (Ron) used to write on my calendar on the last day of the month to get cash at the bank for allowances. Then I would always give it on the first day of the month.

Another "helper" might be a chart on your mirror or refrigerator or even a note to yourself in your checkbook. Perhaps a "foolproof" way would be to give the children the responsibility and freedom to remind you on a set day of the month that the allowance is going to be due in one or two days. You could even assess yourself a late fee as a penalty!

Principles

Two underlying principles are important in overcoming this challenge.

First, habits take time to develop, and giving the allowance must become a habit. Therefore, you have to help yourself establish the habit.

Second, giving the allowance should be as important to you as any other financial transaction. Because of what you're attempting to teach your children, it's as important to pay an allowance on a regular basis as it is to make the mortgage payment. The only difference is that your children aren't likely to foreclose on you if you fail to give them their money.

Challenge: Friends Getting More Money Than Your Kids Do

The seven-year-old down the street gets five dollars per week and our seven-year-old gets one dollar per week.

Potential Solutions

Try the following sequence of steps.

1. Gather your facts. Are your children telling the whole story about their friends' allowances? If you know the parent down the street well enough, you may want to verify the information.

2. Be willing to reevaluate the amount you're giving your children.

3. Help your kids feel they're part of the process of evaluation and reevaluation.

4. If you still feel you're doing exactly as you should after gathering the facts and reevaluating the budget, be firm in your decision. Don't succumb to pressure.

Principles

Inequity is a challenge each of us deals with every day of our lives. Except for the richest person in the world, there will *always* be others with more money.

Succumbing to the pressure of what others do is *not* a money challenge; it's a values and self-discipline challenge. You, as a family, will have certain values that are reflected in the way you spend money. Someone else may have different values, but that doesn't make the different values right.

That's why it's important to be firm in your decisions. Spending because others spend is never wise.

Solving this particular challenge may be the greatest teaching opportunity you have. Don't overlook the opportunity by caving in to the pressure from your children.

Challenge: The "Spender"

How do I handle my child who wastes his money? He never seems to have any money left, and he puts pressure on us to give him extra money between his allowances.

Potential Solutions

The envelope system (Chapter 4) is probably the most effective way to cope with the spender child. It makes a child responsible for his own behavior; therefore, if he's frivolous with his money, he alone will bear the consequences of his actions.

It's a great temptation to give your child more money when he's broke. It sure helps to avoid conflict, but at what price? We've seen plenty of parents who are "stuck" giving money to grown children who always seem "broke."

Principles

As we've stated previously, you must give children the freedom to fail. You must allow them to bear the consequences of their own decisions.

It's better that "spender" children learn this lesson now in the little things—before they become adults.

Challenge: The "Hoarder"

How do I handle a child who won't spend her money? We give our daughter money for refreshments before trips—to the county fair, for example. But instead of spending the money for something to drink, even when she's thirsty, she asks other family members for a sip from their drinks!

Potential Solutions

We're sure many parents would like to have this problem; the spender child is the more common challenge. But hoarding is a very real issue, especially when money isn't spent on the need for which it was given.

The "government approach" may best solve the challenge of hoarding. In setting its budgets for departments and agencies on a year-to-year basis, the government will reduce the following year's budget by any amount left unspent at the end of the current year. As a consequence, the departments and agencies are motivated to spend everything in the budget before the end of the year.

This technique should work with a child by reducing the amount she'll get in the next month, or year, by any amounts left. To ensure that she doesn't "cheat" the system, you may have to require an accounting of where the money has been spent.

Principles

Try to determine why the child won't spend. Probably the challenge is not money. It may well be a desire for security. It could also be an attitude problem, in the sense of selfishly hoarding.

The classic story in the Bible dealing with this tells of the rich fool who built barns and hoarded grain to no avail (see Luke 12:16-21). His perspective was entirely "mine, mine, mine" instead of "This is God's; how can I best use these resources?"

Try to teach that money is a tool, not an end in itself. It's to be used, not just saved. It should be viewed as a resource used to accomplish a goal.

Challenge: Grandparents Giving Large Gifts to Children

My parents give our kids very expensive toys and other gifts that we would not, or could not, give. Many times my parents will give our children anything they want regardless of how many similar items our kids already have.

My husband and I feel this interference often undermines our authority as parents and may damage our effectiveness in training our children to be financially responsible. They feel that they have a "right" to spoil their grandchildren, that this is how grandparents are "supposed" to behave. When I brought the topic up, they implied that I had no basis to interfere with this "right" in any way. What can we do?

Potential Solutions

We recommend picking one or more of the following alternatives.

1. The first and best is to lovingly confront the grandparents with what they're doing. Do this after you have a teaching system, such as the envelope system, in place so that the *system* establishes the standard—not you, and certainly not your parents. Perhaps you can even ask them to participate with you in the system. By doing so you may be able to point out the behavior that's challenging you.

2. A second idea is to present the grandparents with an alternative to the large gift. For example, you could ask them to set up savings accounts for your children instead of giving presents. At some point your kids could share with their grandparents how they used the total of the gifts given to them. Or you could ask your parents to put the money in a college fund. You could also ask them to spend time, rather than money, on your children. A relationship with grandparents is a blessing kids can never purchase.

3. The grandparents could choose to give gifts, but you would have a *limit* on the *amount* spent on the gifts. That way you won't take away the pleasure they get out of giving, and they won't thwart what you want to teach.

4. You may wish to provide a list of needs (school supplies, clothes, etc.) to the grandparents. This may help them give more practical gifts instead of a fifteenth stuffed animal or twentieth doll.

5. Another alternative is to say on your children's behalf, "No, thank you," and return the gift. There is obviously great risk in choosing this alternative in terms of the relationship with the

grandparents, but it may be the only one that meets your objective—teaching your children wisdom.

This method is to be used only when you've tried everything else and your children's well-being is at stake. Be careful not to put your children in an adversarial relationship with their grandparents. It's not the children's fault.

Principles

Unfortunately, there's no easy solution to this challenge. It will most likely come down to what's most important to you—your children's well-being, your relationship with your parents, or the principle involved. If the children's well-being is at stake, it may be worth risking the relationship in order to ensure their healthy development.

A relationship with grandparents is certainly one to be treasured and cultivated. But when it keeps your children from learning the principles of a successful and godly life, or if it undermines your parental authority, you may need to stand firm. If it's a matter of principle, you must decide if you want to risk the relationship for the principle.

Challenge: Wanting Your Children to Do as You Say—Not as You Do

There are many things I do, or don't do, that I don't want my kids to learn. I don't tithe regularly; I don't save enough; I have never budgeted; I don't balance my checkbook; I spend impulsively; and I overuse my credit cards. How can I teach my children not to do these things, when for years they've seen the financial mess I'm in?

Potential Solutions

Granted, none of us is perfect. But a pint of example is worth a gallon of advice.

We discuss this challenge and its importance in more detail in Chapter 2, "Walking the Walk." To summarize, you need to do the following:
1. Confess your failures to your children.
2. Ask for their forgiveness.
3. Accept God's forgiveness.
4. Read *The New Master Your Money* book and complete the workbook to get the basics of money management.
5. Change your behavior one step at a time.

Principles
The first principle underlying this challenge is forgiveness. God has forgiven us through Jesus Christ. You, in turn, need to accept His forgiveness and forgive others.

The second principle is that God will do His part to change your behavior if you do your part. Your part consists of taking steps in obedience to His direction; His part is to provide the power to do so, as He has promised. God has given us His Holy Spirit to enable us to be all He calls us to be.

Your part can begin with a commitment to remember that God owns it all. Then you must exercise enough self-discipline to develop a spending, saving, and tithing plan.

Our challenge to you is to determine what the first step should be; take the step and watch God work in your life and in your children's lives. Don't try to hide your failures from your children; they know far more than you want them to know.

Challenge: A Child with Special Needs

One of our children is especially gifted in sports. Is it fair to treat this child differently from her brothers and sisters? If we give her extra money for sports equipment and other expenses, for example, should her siblings get a similar amount to use as they would like?

Potential Solutions

The answer to this challenge is simple, but the application is difficult: Love your children equally, but treat them uniquely.

No child will ever be equal in every way to brothers or sisters or anyone else. Parents don't have to treat all their kids equally. What's important is that you treat each of your children with justice and fairness and that you *love* them equally.

One way to deal with this challenge is to prepare a budget for each child with his or her help, according to that child's needs. When kids are part of the process, they're more likely to be convinced that it's fair.

Principles

The Bible is clear that we're all uniquely created, even twins.

God loves us all, but doesn't treat us as one group following the same plan. He formed us uniquely and individually. At times He "sets one apart" to be used in different ways to bring Him glory.

Challenge: Handling the "Spender" Along with the Good Money Manager

Among our three children, we have one who's an excellent money manager. But the other two are spenders. How can we treat them equitably? Should we reward or punish them monetarily?

Potential Solutions

Children are naturally going to be different from one another. In the Blue family of five children, we see five different personalities with five different ways of viewing and managing money. It's not a matter of age or gender of the children.

The envelope system frees you to train your kids as unique individuals. The system becomes the standard and the tool, and it helps you communicate that you're on their team, making the system work.

We wouldn't suggest additional rewards or punishment. Benefits will naturally flow to the good money manager anyway as a result of good decisions. Likewise, one who spends unwisely will reap the consequences. You don't need to magnify them further.

Principles
Realize that individual views are not necessarily right or wrong. Saving money is not always better than spending. Recognize that each child is unique and that money is a tool to be used by God to accomplish character development.

Good stewardship is the goal in training your children—not that they spend their money the same way.

Challenge: Giving Kids Too Much

When my sister and I were growing up, our parents gave us whatever we wanted. Somehow, I gradually learned to be a good money manager, but my sister did not. She married a man who can't afford to give her whatever she wants. Their marriage suffers because she learned to equate love with being able to have whatever she wanted. I notice that I'm often lenient with my children. How can I prevent spoiling them?

Potential Solutions
Your sister is a reminder of the price to be paid for the lack of self-discipline on your parents' part. The solution to the problem is found by asking yourself, "Why do I continually give in to my children? Is it because I feel guilty? Is it because I don't want my children to experience the hard times I did?"

What are you teaching them by being so lenient? Probably that there are "no limits" or that it's possible to "buy love." You may even be improving their manipulation skills by allowing them to talk you into buying whatever they want. Remind yourself and them of two sweet fruits of the Spirit: self-control and patience.

The way to deal with the challenge is to determine whether your kids are asking for money because of an inadequate budget. If the answer to that is no, then consider creating earning opportunities for them. Consider the "hiring" activities in Chapter 11. Encourage them to start their own business as shown in the same chapter. We don't recommend giving an advance on their allowance.

It's okay for you to have the freedom to give spontaneously, as long as your kids don't come to expect it.

A couple heard our description of the envelope training system, and implemented it with their four children. A few weeks later they were shopping at a mall. The mother suggested they all get a cookie.

The youngest child broke into tears. Asked why, he replied, "I don't want to spend my money on a cookie."

The mother wisely said, "No, honey, you don't understand. This is my treat." After she said that, the children's eyes brightened as the mother purchased the cookies.

These children really appreciated that treat. Without a money management system, would it have really been appreciated? How many of us have thought about helping our children to be grateful?

Another friend said it this way: "Until there is a limit, there is no value to money." He also shared with us that until he and his wife had set up a budget for their children, they didn't realize how much they were actually giving their kids with a few dollars here and a few dollars there.

Principles

There is a limited supply of money. Children and adults both need to learn this truth and use what they do have wisely and with a thankful heart.

Challenge: The Child Who Plays One Parent Against the Other

Our kids generally know which parent is "softer" for various requests. (We suspect they talk and pool their insights.) How do we keep them from playing off the other or manipulating the softer one?

Potential Solutions

It's pretty common for one parent to be firmer than the other. The challenge occurs when a child actively and knowingly plays one parent against the other.

If Dad tells a child she can't have extra money for the mall, she may ask Mom, hoping for a different answer. Or, in the case of divorced parents, a child may threaten to move out and live with the other parent if he doesn't get his way in money matters.

The solution to this challenge is similar to the one for the challenge of overindulgent grandparents. First, confirm your child's actions with the other parent. Then confront the child.

You can hope that when confronted, the child will change behavior. If, however, he will not change, our advice is twofold: Don't play "the game" and get caught in the trap; and don't take the conflict out on the child.

Consider imposing a "manipulation" penalty (loss of privilege, a fine, etc.) whenever the child asks another parent the same question that one parent has already answered.

Principles

If you're doing your part by being a role model and training your child to manage money, you're fulfilling your responsibility. You may not see the results in the child in the short term, but in the longer term God is faithful.

Commit your child to God. Trust that He will work in your child's life, in His timing. It won't be easy, but we believe your financial training is well worth the commitment and faith required.

Challenge: The Careless Child

Our child continually loses books, jackets, and sweaters (really basic things), and we frequently have to replace them out of our money. If we don't, she may get cold, do poorly in school, or suffer in other ways.

Potential Solutions

Our advice is simply this: Don't take on a responsibility that is the child's.

In other words, don't feel obligated to replace with your money what she lost. If you feel you have to replace whatever it is, at least require her to pay for it out of the next month's allowance or require her to earn the money to pay for it.

You may want to consider an escalating penalty. For example, the first time she loses her jacket, you'll help her find it or replace it.

The second time, she'll have to replace it and compensate you for the time taken in looking for the jacket.

The third time, you may also make her pay you a taxi rate to drive her back to school or church to look for the jacket.

If these recommendations sound harsh, use another loss-of-privilege or loss-of-reward method. You could give her $10 in quarters or an envelope of $1 bills on the first of the month. Every time she loses her jacket or some other possession, she loses a dollar or a quarter from the envelope or jar. She can then keep whatever is left over at the end of the month. We've found this to be very effective in establishing habits.

Principles

We're all responsible for our own actions, and must bear the consequences of those actions. If parents continually step in and remove any consequences for actions, the child may never learn this most important principle.

Challenge: Giving to Your Children Out of a Sense of Guilt

I'm a divorced father who frequently travels out of town on business. Out of guilt, I spend too much on my kids trying to "make up." I can see it's harmful to them and certainly harmful to my finances.

Potential Solutions

Many parents give to their children out of a sense of guilt for over-working, too much travel, or some important "commitment" that keeps them from being with the children. In essence, these moms and dads are attempting to pay for the lack of time or attention.

We aren't equipped to offer professional psychological advice. If you believe that you're dealing with a sense of guilt, you should seek help in Christian counseling. The symptom may be a financial challenge, but the root cause is far more complex.

This must be solved for your sake and for the children's sake. You can't buy love or pay for a wrong suffered.

Challenge: A Child Who Is Getting Ready to Make a Really Stupid Decision

My teenager has saved his money but wants to spend a large portion of it on something very foolish. Should I stop him?

Potential Solutions

Wouldn't it be nice if we could attach a disclaimer to our children that says, "The opinions expressed and the decisions made by this child are not necessarily those of his parents"?

Since children frequently learn financial maturity at the cost of their mistakes, it's often difficult for parents to know just when to step in and forestall the consequences of their child's bad decision.

We understand the essence of your question: How far do you go in allowing a child the freedom to fail? The answer depends on several things. First, how serious is the mistake going to be? For example, allowing a child to spend a dollar foolishly at the arcade is far different from allowing him or her to purchase an unsafe auto-mobile. One child may want to wear name-brand shirts or jeans, whereas another places a higher value on a stereo system.

It also depends on the age of the child and where he is in the learning process. You're certainly going to want to give much more advice at an earlier age than you will later on.

"Stepping in" and "giving advice" are two different things. If you "step in," you stop him from making a mistake by forcing the issue and not allowing him to fail. "Advising" him before he makes the decision and then allowing him to choose is something entirely different.

Deciding when to step in and when to give advice is a judgment call. Examine the situation to see which is an appropriate response. God will give you the wisdom to make the right decision if you ask Him for it (James 1:5).

We're very free with our advice to our children. Sometimes we don't even wait to be asked. But we do let them know that we won't love them any less if they choose against our advice. We try to help them see beforehand that they'll have to live with the choice they make. When they understand the long-term implications of a choice, and that our love is not dependent upon their choosing what we would choose, they experience freedom and security in their decision.

Principles

Our children's choices on how to spend their money often don't match ours. But different isn't always wrong.

Our kids' choices reflect their personalities. Let each child be free to express himself through his choices, assuming they're scripturally sound. Your child's confidence and self-respect will grow as he realizes he can make decisions that are different from those you would make.

Challenge: The Too-Generous Giver

I'm pleased that my child is generous, but she wants to give all of her money away. My husband and I don't want to thwart her generous desires, but we want her to be practical and a good saver.

Potential Solutions

Generally, it's preferable to have a child who's more prone to give than to be selfish. For most of us, selfishness and greed tend to be natural. But we've seen cases, particularly with younger children, of kids who want to give away everything.

My (Jeremy's) daughters have exhibited this quality from time to time. When our younger girl was six years old, she'd saved nine dollars. At our church, Russian missionaries talked about the difficult circumstances they endured. They spoke of people in their church who didn't have enough money to buy coal for heat in the winter.

Our church decided to collect money for the missionaries to take back to their congregation. Our daughter wanted to give all nine dollars to the coal offering. At first we thought we should discourage her from giving it all away; after all, it wouldn't be "practical" for her to give 100 percent of her savings.

We finally decided it was an important opportunity for her to respond to what God was saying through missionaries, so we allowed her to give. As she's grown and matured, she's continued to give—though not 100 percent of savings. We can see that extreme generosity is tempered over time.

Our older daughter used most of the earnings from her craft business to give her sister a surprise gift. Once again, our first impulse was to stop and counsel her about a gift that used up 80 percent of her profits. We realized, however, that our older daughter's "love language" is gift giving. Though she and her sister had argued from time to time, she wished to show love by giving a gift with her own money.

We allowed this, and it helped to improve the relationship. She hasn't continued to give the same amount every year, but felt led to at that particular time.

Principles

As many preachers have reminded us, "You can't outgive God." As He does for the lowly sparrows or the wildflowers of the field, He will provide.

Though giving very generously may reduce one's ability to buy every luxury, we're still confident He will meet genuine needs. As Paul told the Corinthians, "Remember this: Whoever sows sparingly will also reap sparingly, and whoever sows generously will also reap generously" (2 Corinthians 9:6).

Challenge: Letting Them Use Credit Cards Without Getting into Trouble

If I'm to teach my kids all about money, it would seem that they need to have a credit card to understand. We don't want to advocate debt, but you must have a credit card these days to purchase items on the Internet, to rent cars, to travel, and so on. Should I give them my credit card or their own?

Potential Solutions

We wouldn't recommend giving your kids your card the next time they go to the mall with their friends or when they travel. The temptation to overspend is too great.

A practical alternative may be a "secured" card or a stored-value card. These are not technically credit cards. They're like a prepaid calling card with a preset limit. Parents decide the amount to prepay. When the balance is zero, the teen is automatically cut off.

An example of this card is the Visa Buxx. The cardholder must be at least age 13 and some service charges may apply.

Principles

Most kids don't have the maturity to handle credit cards responsibly. Credit cards are a vital part of adult life. So are driving and sex, but that doesn't mean your 14-year-old is mature enough for either one.

A recent study found that 11 percent of teenagers under 18 have credit cards. A whopping 76 percent of college undergraduate students carry the plastic; 43 percent of those college students have four or more cards.[3]

Your kids will have plenty of opportunities to learn hands-on. For now, they'll learn what they need to know by watching you use credit cards wisely and by hearing you discuss their best use "as you go." There's no need to "build a credit record" at young ages. Getting credit is not very difficult these days.

Summary of Activities

Trait	Activity Name	Page	Teaching Goals	Age Range
Generous Giver	Charity Gifts for Birthday Parties	96	Reducing dependency on material gifts for happiness; encouraging others to give; teaching leverage in giving; allowing children to directly give to a charity or ministry	8-14
	Head Up a Giving Foundation	98	Allowing kids to decide a portion of the family's giving budget; experiencing the joy of giving more substantial amounts; practicing the decision-making process	6-18
	Candy, Dolls, Army Men, and Proportions	101	Illustrating the prosperity and relative material advantage your children may enjoy; increasing appreciation for blessings; motivating sharing and giving out of abundance	4-12
	The Blessing List: an Anti-Envy Tool	104	Counting blessings; not taking blessings for granted; defending against envy and coveting	6-18

Trait	Activity Name	Page	Teaching Goals	Age Range
Generous Giver	Plan a Family Mission Project	107	Giving time and service in addition to money; seeing and meeting people in less fortunate circumstances; appreciating blessings	8-18
	Matching Gift Program	110	Leveraging money to support important causes; giving intentionally; tracking gifts given	8-18
	Read Books, Watch Videos about Giving	112	Inspiring kids toward generous giving and philanthropy	Various
Sharp Shopper	Currency Exchange	118	Appreciating the value of a dollar; understanding relative value by converting the cost of items into work units or allowance units	8-18
	Buying Consultant	120	Allowing children to express the wisdom they've gained about making purchases; holding them accountable to their own advice	8-16

Trait	Activity Name	Page	Teaching Goals	Age Range
Sharp Shopper	How Much Does It Really Cost?	122	Adding up the total cost of a purchase including interest; improving discernment in making financial decisions	10-18
	Advertising Detectives	124	Discerning the aims of advertising; thinking through the arguments of the advertising pitch	7-14
	Food Court Funding	127	Allocating spending within boundaries; making minor decisions	8-16
	Compare Product Labels	129	Understand labels and the value offered by private brands; seeing that products with the same ingredients have different prices	8-14
	Conduct a Taste Test	133	Judging quality and price differences between leading brands and less expensive ones	4-10
	Brainstorming Before Buying	134	Providing alternatives to buying; thinking of creative solutions to needs	7-15

Trait	Activity Name	Page	Teaching Goals	Age Range
Sharp Shopper	Treasure Hunt for Change	136	Understanding different coins and their value	3-8
	Coin Combo Platter Game	138	Knowing what coins are worth; improving counting abilities	5-10
	Trust…but Cut the Cards	140	Counting and verifying correct change	5-10
	Read Sharp Shopping Books and Watch a Video	141	Motivating children to be sharp shoppers	3-12
Savvy Saver	Piggy Banking	146	Generating interest in saving; allocating among categories of saving, spending, and giving	3-10
	Picture Your Savings Goal	148	Setting savings goals; providing motivation for delaying gratification	6-12
	Family 401(k)	150	Beginning the habit of regular saving and investing; setting up longer-term savings and specifying in advance the conditions for withdrawals	10-18

Trait	Activity Name	Page	Teaching Goals	Age Range
Savvy Saver	"Let's Make a Money Deal" Game Show	153	Illustrating the powerful effects of compounding interest; sharpening math skills	10-18
	Opportunity Knocks	155	Understanding the opportunity cost of consuming today instead of saving	12-18
	Matching Short-Term Savings Goals	157	Providing incentives to help your child save for specific purposes	6-16
	Play Math Computer Games	159	Sharpening math skills in an entertaining way	4-12
	Making Savings More "Interest"-ing	161	Illustrating the idea of money earning interest	4-10
	Read Savvy Saver Books	162	Convincing your child to be a regular saver	Various
Prudent Planner	Give Some, Save Some, Spend Some	166	Developing the habit of dividing earnings among saving, giving, and spending categories	3-10

Trait	Activity Name	Page	Teaching Goals	Age Range
Prudent Planner	Treasure Trackers	167	Forming the habit of tracking money and reconciling accounts	5-9
	The Time-and-Money Coupon Gift	170	Allocating limited financial resources among unlimited alternatives; planning and scheduling an event with a predetermined budget	8-18
	Birthday Date and Goal Setting	173	Guiding children in setting goals	8-18
	Driving and Car Contract	175	Remembering the responsibility that accompanies privileges	15-18
	Object Lesson: Money and Bills	179	Showing where the money comes from and where it goes; planning spending so you have enough for basic needs	4-12
	Paying the Bills for a Month	181	Understanding monthly living expenses; training in everyday, adult financial matters	12-18

Trait	Activity Name	Page	Teaching Goals	Age Range
Prudent Planner	Celebrating Financial Freedom	182	Making decisions and living with the consequences; describing your future levels of financial support	18-24
	Read Books Showing the Wisdom of Prudent Planning	185	Persuading children to be prudent planners	Various
Intelligent Investor	The Gambling Fool Simulator	187	Illustrating the foolishness of gambling and how unlikely winning the lottery is	10-18
	Candy Day	190	Establishing early patterns of delayed gratification, important for investing; preventing "spoiling" of kids; setting boundaries	2-10
	Corn Kernels and the Power of Investing	192	Illustrating the multiplying effect of investment; showing the risks	4-14
	The Rule of 72	194	Providing a quick way to calculate how long it takes an investment to double with compounding	10-18

Trait	Activity Name	Page	Teaching Goals	Age Range
Intelligent Investor	Play Monopoly	195	Learning truths about investing, real estate returns, and risk through a "hands-on" approach	8-18
	Play Cashflow for Kids	198	Managing personal cash flow; understanding more complex financial terms and concepts	6-14
	Investment Activity to Track Stocks	200	Practicing investment in the stock market; learning about potential returns and risks	9-16
	Buy One Share of Stock	202	Providing a tangible experience of owning stock in a company	8-14
	Read Books for Intelligent Investing	203	Convincing children to set aside money so its value can grow	Various
Willing Worker	Hire Your Children at Home	206	Providing opportunities to earn money; recognizing the effort it takes	6-18
	Hire Your Children at Your Business	208	Providing work experience; paying allowances in a tax-efficient way	8-18

Trait	Activity Name	Page	Teaching Goals	Age Range
Willing Worker	Job Contract	209	Defining and agreeing on boundaries for your child's work outside the home	12-18
	Become a Business Incubator	211	Encouraging children to start a business and meet needs; understanding basic operations of a business	9-18
	Profits and Payback	213	Grasping the true costs of having a business	10-18
	Read Willing Worker Books	215	Building a good work ethic; reinforcing the value and benefits of work	Various

Notes

Chapter 1

1. Bill Cosby, *Kids Say the Darndest Things* (New York: Bantam Books, 1998), p. 59.
2. Money Savvy Generation Web site at www.msgen.com.
3. *Money* magazine, September 2004.
4. Lewis Mandelle, Ph.D., conducted the 2004 annual study by Jump$tart Coalition titled "Financial Literacy: Are We Improving?" surveying 4,000 high school seniors in 350 schools.
5. National Council on Economic Education, "Survey of the States: Economic and Personal Finance Education in Our Nation's Schools in 2004: A Report Card," March 2005, p. 3.
6. "Sex Education in America: Principals Survey," January 2004. Study jointly completed by Harvard University, Kaiser Family Foundation, and National Public Radio.
7. National Consumers League, March/April 2002 NCL Bulletin, www.nclnet.org.
8. Remarks by Chairman Alan Greenspan at the 33rd Annual Legislative Conference of the Congressional Black Caucus, Washington, D.C., September 26, 2003.

Chapter 2

1. www.thevandels.com/kidsay.html.
2. Robert Frick, Ph.D., "The Jukes-Edwards Story: Truth and Myth of Max Jukes," found at www.rfrick.info/jukes.htm. The study of "Max Juke" was conducted by Richard Dugdale; the report on Jonathan Edwards was prepared by A.E. Winship.

Chapter 3

1. Laura Jereski, "Shirtsleeves to Shirtsleeves," *Forbes* magazine, October 21, 1991, p. 34.
2. Erik Hurst and Kerwin Kofi Charles, "The Correlation of Wealth across Generations," *Journal of Political Economy*, University of Chicago Press, 2003, Volume 111(6), pp. 1155-1182.
3. "As Rich-Poor Gap Widens in the U.S., Class Mobility Stalls," *Wall Street Journal*, May 13, 2005, pp. A-1 and A-7.

Chapter 4

1. Dr. James Dobson, *Complete Marriage and Family Home Reference Guide* (Wheaton, IL: Tyndale House Publishers, 2000), pp. 84-85.

Chapter 5

1. Cosby, *Kids Say the Darndest Things*, p. 86.

Chapter 7

1. http://rinkworks.com/said/kidquotes.shtml.
2. www.toothpasteworld.com/choosing.htm.

Chapter 8

1. Information used with permission from the Piggy Bank Page (http://www.piggybankpage.co.uk/), a Web site devoted to the collecting of valuable piggy banks as art.
2. William L. Anthes, "Financial Illiteracy in America: A Perfect Storm, a Perfect Opportunity," *Journal of Financial Service Professionals*, November 2004, pp. 49-56.
3. Greenspan, 33rd Annual Legislative Conference of the Congressional Black Caucus.

Chapter 10

1. Charles T. Clotfelter and Philip J. Cook, *Selling Hope* (Cambridge, MA: Harvard University Press, 1989), p. 11.
2. Richard C. Leone, "High Stakes: Substance Abuse and Gambling," 2001 speech at CASA conference.
3. Tyler J. Jarvis, "Gambling—What Are the Odds," *BYU Magazine*, Spring 2001, Volume 55, No. 1, p. 50.
4. www.powerball.com.

Chapter 11

1. Cosby, *Kids Say the Darndest Things*, p. 49.
2. www.nbia.org.

Chapter 12

1. Cosby, *Kids Say the Darndest Things*, p. 79.
2. 2003 survey by Yankelovich Youth Monitor, in Jonathan Clements, "Teach Your Children Wealth: Why I Decided to Close Down the Bank of Dad," *Wall Street Journal*, October 15, 2003, p. D1.
3. JA Worldwide survey as published in *Wall Street Journal*, June 1, 2005, p. D1.

Glossary

Allowance – A specific amount of money a parent gives a child regularly as a benefit of being a family member.

Appreciation – An increase in fair market value of an asset.

Assets – Everything a person owns, including cash, investments, business, land, and house. It includes physical, tangible assets as well as intangible assets.

Balance sheet – A condensed financial statement showing the amount and nature of an individual's assets and liabilities at a given time. A "snapshot" of what a person owns and what he owes. Sometimes referred to as a net worth statement.

Bank – An institution where money may be safely kept and which lends money and provides other financial services.

Beneficiary – One who is designated to receive a benefit; for example, the person who would receive the proceeds of a life insurance settlement.

Bond – A promise of a corporation, municipality, government, church, etc., to pay interest at a stated rate and repay face value of a certificate. It is a loan from you to the organization to mature at a specified date.

Budget – A plan or guideline for spending.

Check – A written order to a bank to pay a specified amount of money to a specific person or company from money on deposit with the bank.

Chore – A routine task performed around the home.

Credit – Money loaned, usually for a fee, that must be paid back later.

Credit card – A plastic device that allows people to borrow and make purchases which are paid for over a period of time.

Debit card – A plastic device that allows retailers to draw funds directly from a consumer's bank account in order to make purchases.

Debt – The money you owe when you buy on credit or borrow from someone else.

Diversification – Spreading money among different types of investments to limit your overall risk.

Dividends – The profits that a company distributes to its owners, or stockholders.

Federal Reserve Bank – Neither an actual bank nor a government agency, it was created in 1913 by Congress to stabilize the nation's economy. The Federal Reserve Bank is the central bank of the United States and is owned by all the member banks. It is divided into 12 regional banks that are spread across the country. The bank's main work is to control the supply of money. It holds a percentage of the funds (the reserves) of commercial banks and lends money to them when needed.

Individual Retirement Account (IRA) – A tax-deferred account used to save money for future retirement and receive tax advantages. A traditional IRA provides an immediate tax deduction and grows tax-deferred. Taxes are paid when the traditional IRA is distributed. A Roth IRA provides no immediate tax deduction, but all the growth in value is tax-free. There are no taxes when the Roth IRA is distributed within applicable restrictions.

Inflation – An economic condition characterized by rising prices, usually caused by too much available money in the economy.

Inheritance – Assets, usually money or other forms of property, passed on to an individual after the death of another person.

Interest – The cost to rent or use money. Borrowers pay interest to rent money from a lender. Savers receive interest from banks wanting to rent the savers' money.

Investment – The use of money for the purpose of making more money; to gain income, increase capital, save taxes, or a combination of the three.

Liabilities – Claims against you; obligations you owe. Some may be current (owed within the year), such as credit card loans;

others may be long-term, such as a home mortgage.

Liquidity (liquid) – The state of assets readily converted to cash at their current fair market value. A liquid asset will not lose value upon its sale as a result of a lack of a ready market.

Living expenses – The total cost of your lifestyle. The amount of money to provide for your home, transportation, and other necessities.

Long-term assets (nonliquid) – Those assets that cannot easily be converted to cash or sold or consumed in a short period of time. Examples: a family business, a home, and land assets.

Money – Anything a group of people accepts in exchange for goods or services.

Mortgage – Usually refers to the balance of the loan on a home. Also the amount of money borrowed to purchase a home.

Mutual fund – A pooling of money by many people to be invested by professional investment managers in stocks and bonds.

Nonliquid – Assets not easily converted to cash at their current fair market value.

Offerings – Money that is given to a charity or ministry.

Savings – Money that is stored safely so that it can be used later.

Stock – A certificate showing ownership of a company.

Stockbroker – One who advises on which stocks or bonds to buy, and who buys them on a client's behalf. Sometimes called financial advisors, financial planners, or financial representatives, they may also provide mutual funds and annuities.

Stockholder – A person who owns stock (shares) in a company.

Stock market – The place where shares of many different companies are bought and sold.

Tithe – One tenth of a person's income, usually given to support a church.

Will – The legal statement of a person's wishes concerning how his property will be divided and minor children cared for after the person's death.

Withholding – Refers to the amount of tax reserved from a paycheck.

RON BLUE

Ron is the author of more than a dozen books on personal finance from a biblical perspective, including the bestselling *Master Your Money*, *Wealth To Last*, (co-authored with Larry Burkett), and *Splitting Heirs*. He is featured in the popular *Master Your Money* video series. A frequent guest on numerous radio and television programs, he is also a regular contributor to several national Christian magazines.

In addition, Ron is president of the Christian Financial Professionals Network (CFPN), an international effort to equip and motivate Christian financial professionals to serve the body of Christ. He has served on the board of directors of many Christian organizations, including Campus Crusade for Christ, Crown Financial Ministries, the Family Research Council, Promise Keepers, and Walk Thru the Bible Ministries.

Following his graduation from Indiana University with a Masters of Business Administration degree, Ron joined the management group of Peat, Marwick, Mitchell & Co. and worked with the firm in New York City, Dallas, and San Francisco. After founding an Indianapolis-based certified public accounting firm that has grown to be one of the 50 largest in the United States, he became Administrative Vice President of Leadership Dynamics International—where he developed and taught biblically-based leadership and management seminars in the U.S. and Africa.

Ron then founded a firm that offered financial planning with a biblical worldview; it grew to manage over $2 billion in assets for more than 5,000 clients nationwide. He retired from that company in 2003 to lead the Christian Financial Professionals Network.

Ron and his wife, Judy, live in Atlanta. They have five children and seven grandchildren.

JUDY BLUE

As a wife, mother, author, and teacher, Judy Blue has a heart for teaching and encouraging women of all ages. A popular speaker at seminars and retreats, she has spent 25 years discipling women—including a five-year stint leading a weekly Bible study for nearly a hundred young mothers.

Judy's books, co-authored with her husband, Ron, include *Raising Money Smart Kids, A Woman's Guide to Financial Peace of Mind,* and *Money Talks and So Can We.* She enjoys ministering to women and challenging them to think rightly about themselves and God.

God also has given her a ministry of helping families and individuals understand the relationship between nutrition and disease. Judy earned her B.S. and M.S. degrees from Indiana University. Today she and Ron enjoy frequent visits with their adult children and grandchildren.

JEREMY WHITE

Jeremy has been a Certified Public Accountant for nearly 20 years with financial experience in public accounting and industry. Currently a partner in Blythe, White & Associates, a certified public accounting and consulting firm, he has assisted with several best-selling financial books. They include *The New Master Your Money* and *Splitting Heirs,* both written with Ron Blue. Jeremy also wrote with Ron Blue and the late Larry Burkett the bestselling *Wealth to Last: Money Essentials for the Second Half of Life.*

Jeremy has been a contributor for five years to Larry Burkett's *Money Matters* newsletter. He also assisted Larry Burkett and Crown Financial Ministries as the primary writing consultant in updating their successful workbook, *Family Financial Planning.* He has been a frequent guest on Crown Financial Ministries' "How to Manage Your Money" radio broadcast.

Before founding his financial firm, Jeremy worked with the national accounting firm of Ernst & Young in its Miami office. He is a member of the Christian Financial Professionals Network.

Jeremy's company provides tax preparation, business consulting, estate planning, and personal financial planning services. For more information, see his Web site at www.blythewhite.com.

Jeremy and his wife, Sharon, live in Paducah, Kentucky where they homeschool their two daughters, Jenaye and Jaclyn.

"Our advisors are called to make a difference"

Ron Blue
CFPN President

CFPN™
CERTIFIED

There is a difference in the kind of advice you will receive from a CFPN Certified™ Professional than any other advisor. One of the greatest unrecognized and unmet needs in the body of Christ today is the ability to find a financial professional who shares a Biblical perspective on stewardship. CFPN Certification introduces a new level of qualified, Christian financial professionals who are equipped to integrate Biblical counsel with financial counsel.

CFPN Certification™ qualifies professionals in five specific areas. A CFPN Certified™ Professional:

- is a believer in Jesus Christ.
- adheres to a professional code of ethics.
- personally practices Biblical stewardship.
- is able to integrate Biblical wisdom into their advice and counsel.
- is professionally qualified in one of many disciplines.

These select groups of professionals are not only professionally competent, but are also passionate about their faith.

Visit CFPN.org to find a CFPN Certified™ financial professional near you.

CHRISTIAN FINANCIAL PROFESSIONALS NETWORK

FOCUS ON THE FAMILY®

Welcome to the family!

Whether you purchased this book, borrowed it, or received it as a gift, we're glad you're reading it. It's just one of the many helpful, encouraging, and biblically based resources produced by Focus on the Family for people in all stages of life.

Focus began in 1977 with the vision of one man, Dr. James Dobson, a licensed psychologist and author of numerous best-selling books on marriage, parenting, and family. Alarmed by the societal, political, and economic pressures that were threatening the existence of the American family, Dr. Dobson founded Focus on the Family with one employee and a once-a-week radio broadcast aired on 36 stations.

Now an international organization reaching millions of people daily, Focus on the Family is dedicated to preserving values and strengthening and encouraging families through the life-changing message of Jesus Christ.

Focus on the Family Magazines

These faith-building, character-developing publications address the interests, issues, concerns, and challenges faced by every member of your family from preschool through the senior years.

Focus on the Family
Citizen®
U.S. news issues

Focus on the Family
Clubhouse Jr.™
Ages 4 to 8

Focus on the Family
Clubhouse™
Ages 8 to 12

Breakaway®
Teen guys

Brio®
Teen girls
12 to 16

Brio & Beyond®
Teen girls
16 to 19

Plugged In®
Reviews movies, music, TV

FOR MORE INFORMATION

 Online:
Log on to www.family.org
In Canada, log on to www.focusonthefamily.ca

 Phone:
Call toll free: (800) A-FAMILY (232-6459)
In Canada, call toll free: (800) 661-9800

BP06XFM

More Great Resources
from Focus on the Family®

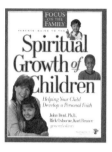

PARENTS' GUIDE TO THE SPIRITUAL GROWTH OF CHILDREN:
Passing on a heritage of faith to children is an incredible privilege God gives to parents. You'll learn how to create a customized plan for your child with fun, faith-filled activities for each stage of development. You'll also learn how to take advantage of the "teachable moments" of everyday life to illustrate spiritual principles. (Paperback and Hardcover.)

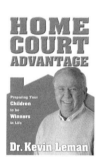

HOME COURT ADVANTAGE:
Many well-meaning parents, hoping to give their children a head start in life, overload their schedules and fragment family time. The result? Hurried childhoods, distant relationships and a failure to pass on vital values. Best-selling author and psychologist Dr. Kevin Leman shows you how to reclaim your role as the primary influence on your child by enjoying time together and making indelible, life-shaping memories. (Hardcover.)

TREND-SAVVY PARENTING:
Baby software or building blocks? If keeping up with the latest trends makes your head spin, *Trend-Savvy Parenting* can help. With practical advice and topics you *need* to understand, trends expert Dr. Mary Manz Simon will enlighten and encourage you as you navigate the current ideas and influences that affect your child. (Hardcover.)

FOR MORE INFORMATION

 Online:
Log on to www.family.org
In Canada, log on to www.focusonthefamily.ca.

 Phone:
Call toll free: (800) A-FAMILY
In Canada, call toll free: (800) 661-9800.

Focus *on the* Family®

BP06XP1